Look at It This Way

Look at It This Way

◆

Focusing on the Feelings of Family and Friends, Clients and Co-workers

John Erik Aho

iUniverse, Inc.
New York Lincoln Shanghai

Look at It This Way
Focusing on the Feelings of Family and Friends, Clients and Co-workers

iUniverse, Inc.

For information address:
iUniverse, Inc.
2021 Pine Lake Road, Suite 100
Lincoln, NE 68512
www.iuniverse.com

ISBN: 0-595-28914-2 (pbk)
ISBN: 0-595-65936-5 (cloth)

Printed in the United States of America

Contents

Introduction

Theodore Roosevelt once said, "The single most important ingredient in the formula of success is knowing how to get along with people." We're all in relationships. At home. At work. At school. What relationship can't stand a little improvement?

Whether I've been a leader in a company or have been led, I saw how managers who spend time developing the relationships with the people around them have an edge over those who don't. I studied the leadership styles of hundreds of leaders when I was on staff with *Insider Business Journal* in Michigan. I have tried to implement those lessons learned in my own leadership as the area director for Young Life here in Napa, California. I also realized that I could be a success in business while blowing it at home. Focusing on the feelings of family and friends, clients and coworkers is the aim of this book. If the relationships around you need improvement then you may want to *look at it this way.*

At work—Customer Satisfaction vs. Customer Loyalty

Chief Executive magazine reported on a roundtable discussion between company leaders. The focus of that discussion was the relationship between client and customer, stating that "one can best anticipate how to delight a customer after developing some degree of intimacy" with them. As suggested by those leaders, the only way companies could develop that level of intimacy was "to liberate their companies' front-line people from purely transaction-based customer relationships."[1]

---

1. J.P. Donlon, "CE Roundtable: Delighting the Customer," *Chief Executive*, June 1997

What came out in the discussion was the difference between customer satisfaction and customer loyalty.

"What really matters is customer loyalty, not satisfaction," said J.P. Donlon, Editor-in-Chief of *Chief Executive*. "Many industries report improving customer satisfaction scores, but this often doesn't translate into continued purchases of products and services. In the auto industry for example, 90 percent of the industry's customers report that they are satisfied to very satisfied. Yet repurchase rates remain stuck in the 35 to 40 percent range."

What does this mean? Your customers may be satisfied with the level of service or the quality of products you provide them, but it may not be enough to keep them loyal to you. We spend millions insuring the quality of our products and services. We also need to spend time insuring the quality of the relationships between our customers, between us and our employees, our co-workers and our families and us.

"If satisfaction to some degree is a smokescreen," Donlon asked, "how can one penetrate the fog of customer relations in order to understand what the customer needs beyond what he or she articulates?" How do you change your customer retention rate from a 35 percent to a 95 percent? In this incredible time of economic prosperity, when it is difficult to find good workers and keep them in our companies, how do we keep our employee retention high? What do we have to do to keep our families together?

Dilip Saraf, whose company, QI International sponsored the *Chief Executive* roundtable, said that "CEOs should ensure that basic requirements are met in order for front-line people to be free to deepen their relationship with customers at all levels, to know best how to exceed expectations and anticipate expressed needs.

"Most of the time employees are dealing with customers on a transactional basis—whether a shipment is delivered, or whether the information has been transmitted. Front-line employees need to get out of the purely transactional domain of following tasks in order to become 'intimate.' Furthermore, everyone in an organization needs to know or be trained in how best to become 'customer-intimate,' assuming one's customers are receptive."

A focus

When you look at the landscape of your life—your family, your company, your community—you can focus on any number of things. Bills that need to be paid. Paperwork that needs to be filled out. Sales that need to be made. Customers that need to be contacted. But beyond all the transactions you can make in a given day, I am calling us to focus on one aspect of our lives that is the most important of all: developing the relationships with the people around us.

A strategy

Just as there are different aspects of our lives we could focus on, there are different ways to look at what we are focusing on. The strategy I want to suggest is to look at the people around you through the lens of focusing on their feelings. For example, does your wife feel like you understand her? Does your husband feel like you respect him? Do your children feel like they are an important part of your life? Do your friends feel like you care about them? Do your co-workers feel they are a part of the team? Do your employees feel empowered? Do your customers feel significant?

By focusing on the feelings of those around you, you will be able to see some of the following results in your life:

1. You will have more rewarding relationships.

2. You will be able to call your spouse your best friend.

3. Your children will feel closer to you.

4. You will find that your employees enjoy working for you.

5. You will exceed the expectations of your customers, because for once, you will know what those expectations are.

6. You will be able to anticipate the needs of your customers because you will be able to tell what they need in the future, not just now.

The feelings to focus on

This is not an exhaustive list. You may come up with other feelings to focus on. Do the people around us feel appreciated? Do they feel competent? Do they feel like they have a sense of direction? Do they feel free to explore new ideas and free to make mistakes? Do they feel loved? Do they feel secure? If you have any other suggestions about feelings to focus on, go to www.LeadershipJourney.com, and tell me what they are. Also, share stories of what others did to make you feel a certain way or what you are doing on your own leadership journey.

The steps

The first step will be to **define the feeling**. The second step will be to discover what it means to feel that way by **walking in their shoes**. In this section I will ask you to take an *i-exam*, where you will examine your focus as a leader. Step three will be to outline a strategy for **developing feeling** in those who follow us, work with us, and live with us.

Leaders who have focused on friendships

Throughout the book are pictures of leaders who are focusing on the friendships around them. We will look into their lives as they share when they have felt appreciated by someone. They will share insights on how they have helped a co-worker feel trusted, a customer feel understood, or a family member feel loved.

The difference an i-exam can make.

As soon as I started my master's work I started to develop headaches. I didn't have them all the time, but I did notice that they were more frequent in California than in Michigan. I thought it had something to do with a new environment until I went home for Christmas break.

I told my mom about my headaches, and she asked a simple question. Moms are good for that, aren't they? After an hour of hunting for something, she would go into the same area, find what I was looking for and say, "Move something." Simple.

"Have you had your eyes checked recently?" she asked. I told her I hadn't, so I made an appointment at the local Eyeglass Factory. As I went through the exam, and as the doctor experimented with different lenses, I realized that I was not seeing all that I could see. I am nearsighted. I see what's closest to me the best. I can't read road signs, or see the details of the woods out my window. I never realized what I was missing.

Near-sighted leadership

Do you realize what you're missing? For some of us it takes extra effort to be far-sighted. It's easier for me to focus on myself than it is to focus on the needs and feelings of others.

Mom asked a simple question. "Have you had your eyes examined?" After the examination, the ophthalmologist prescribed glasses, and they were created within a couple days. And the things I could see! I could read the sign for my exit instead of blowing by it. I could see animals through the woods. I could see colors more brilliantly.

They are simple questions. "Are you focusing on the feelings of others? Do the people around you feel understood?" They are common sense questions. However, if my actions were more common, I would find more fulfilling relationships with those around me.

If I focused more attention on my wife, we would have a happier marriage. If I focused my eyes on the feelings of my girls, I would have a deeper friendship with them. If I focused my sight on my business associates, I would know how to better serve them. If I maintained a closer relationship with my customers, I would be able to assess their present needs and anticipate their future expectations.

What has focusing on the feelings of others done for other leaders?

From unknown to number one

At the age of 27, Danny Meyer started his first restaurant in the heart of New York City. How did a young entrepreneur take his restaurant from being unknown to being number one according to a New York City survey? Meyer got his staff to focus on the feelings of their customers.

"We've tried to distinguish ourselves by going beyond 'customer service'—by offering people hospitality. What's the difference? Service is a technical skill; hospitality is an emotional skill. To me, great service means that the food arrives on time, that the wine is presented properly, and that the plates are cleared gracefully and promptly. But I'd say that a place has great hospitality if you leave there *feeling* that the staff is on your side. It isn't any more complicated than that." (Whenever the emphasis on *feeling* is made, it is usually because I want to drive home the point.)

For Meyer, focusing on the feelings of his customers means having a staff that not only focuses on their product, but also focuses on you. If they overhear you debating between the oxtail and the lamb, they might bring you a small taste of each before you order.

Focusing on your feelings might mean that if you leave your credit card or purse at the restaurant, instead of having you come back and get it, they may have it delivered to you by messenger.

"Although it costs us money to return your belongings," Meyer continued, "it's a great investment. When you realize that you've left something somewhere and that you'll have to schlep back there to get it, it leaves a bad taste in your mouth—even after you've had a wonderful dining experience. So we try to turn what could otherwise become a negative *feeling* into a positive one."

You may not have thought of focusing on someone's feelings in a business relationship, but you can see how it pays off. This focus is what some may call a "soft" skill in leadership. Meyer realized that you can train a waiter how to carry a tray or that coffee should be poured away from the customer instead of on the table.

"Wait staff skills are very trainable; human-being skills are not," Meyer said. "I can train anyone to be knowledgeable about our wine list or how to clear a table properly. But I cannot teach people to care about how their actions affect others. Do your hiring right—that's more than half the battle."[2]

That's what I want to teach in this book. I want to teach you that your actions affect the feelings of those around you. I want to teach what feelings to focus on and how to focus on them. Still not convinced?

From distrust to delight

"Asking people how they *feel,* and responding to them is more important today than it's ever been," said Vera Katz, Portland, Oregon City Mayor, "especially when it comes to government. People have lost a tremendous amount of faith in government. At the local level, we have a great opportunity to help citizens regain that trust. We need to remember that it's citizens who pay our salaries, and they expect accountability from us."

Katz, who was Governing Magazine's Public Official of the Year Award winner in 1994, realized that focusing on the feelings of Portland's 500,000-plus customers would help her restore that trust in government. The city that she has led since 1993 was ranked in the top 10 on Fortune's "Best Cities for Business" list two times. How has Katz focused on the feelings of her citizens?

"The best way to find out how well we're serving our customers…is to ask them. For the past eight years, we've mailed a survey to almost 10,000 citizens, asking them to rate the performance of our police department, our water bureau, our environmental services, our public transportation, and other city bureaus. We also ask our citizens the fol-

---

2.   Lucy McCauley, "How May I Help You?" *Fast Company*, 03–01–2000, pp 93.

lowing questions: Do you *feel* safe walking at night in your neighborhood, in your parks, in your downtown? Are the streets clean enough? What do you think of the city's speed limits? How do you rate the parks and recreation services? And how do you rate the livability of the city?"[3]

Katz then takes those results, matches them up to six other cities, and if Portland is not doing as well as they are, they find out what those cities are doing and implement them in Portland. They mail the results to their citizens, and Katz holds an hour-long television show to go over the results of the survey, all in an effort to focus on the feelings of those around her.

Focusing on the feelings of his customers has made Danny Meyer a success in New York. Focusing on the feelings of her citizens has made Vera Katz a success in Portland. Focusing on the feelings of your family, your friends, your co-workers and your clients will make you a success no matter where you live.

It's time to look over the landscape of our lives, focusing on the friendships around us by focusing on their feelings.

---

3.   Ibid.

1

Do the people around you feel appreciated by you?

○ ○

"To be oppressed is wrong, but to be overlooked may be even worse."

—Max DePree in Leadership Jazz

Dennis Van Norman, a human resources consultant in Minneapolis, told the *Minneapolis Star Tribune:* "When companies talk to me about employee involvement programs, they don't ask, 'How can we involve employees?' They ask, 'How can we make employees *feel* involved?'"

For Van Norman, "Touchy-feely" is dead. Van Norman states that we don't want touching in the modern corporation. These days it's just "feely."

"Employers have been told over and over that employees don't really care about money, what they really want is to *feel* included and appreciated."[1]

I personally don't set out to do something so that others will notice me. But I'll be honest; it sure feels good when they do. It feels great when I hear Michelle tell me that I am a good dad for my children. I like it when I get a letter from a business saying they liked an article I wrote on them. All of us have a need to be recognized.

---

1. Dale Dauten, "Care needed in making employees feel appreciated," *Minneapolis Star Tribune*, 07–23–1997, pp 02D

Define the Feeling

If you feel appreciated, you feel valued and esteemed. Someone has noticed you for who you are or for what you have done. If I appreciate you, I treasure you. You feel like a prized possession. You feel like someone recognizes your worth. To appreciate someone can simply mean to be aware of him or her. Are you aware of the people around you? Do the people around you feel like you are aware of their needs, dreams, and desires?

Walk in Their Shoes

Take a walk. I mean it. After you read this section, put the book down and take a walk. The "walk in their shoes" section of this book is your chance to reflect on what it means to be appreciated. Part of focusing on the feelings of those around you has to do with feeling what it meant when someone focused on you. The following is a set of questions to help you feel what it means to be appreciated.

Please take some time to truly walk in the shoes of other people by answering these questions for yourself. Don't just read. React to what you learn. Interact with what you learn. Act on what you learn.

i-exam

When have I been appreciated?
What have I done that was appreciated?
What is it about my character that people appreciate?
How specific were they in their appreciation of me?
Who appreciates me and how have they shown it?
What does it feel like when I am taken for granted?
Have I ever left a job because I was not appreciated?

Develop the Feeling

It can be scary when *i-exam*ine myself. Sometimes it's easier to look at the negative than the positive about myself. What did you feel? As you looked back on the times when you were recognized for a specific accomplishment, how did that feel? That is what we need to develop in the people around us. How do we do that?

Let's look at a humorous story of how not to do it first. Van Norman was told of a department manager who created an Employee of the Month program in order to improve employee morale. He chose four categories that he would award, but had no budget for the program.

"In an effort to economize, he decided that he didn't need to go out and buy plaques, not when he had, right there in his garage, boxes full of his old bowling trophies. So he dug out his trophies with the little golden bowlers, and pasted paper labels over the little engraved nameplates."

Since Van Norman has discovered such a "hunger for appreciation" in the market place, employees were probably grateful, no matter how tacky the awards were.

Take a time-out

Our most valuable resource is not what we find in our accounts or our wallets. The most valuable resource we have is time, and we need to spend it wisely. If you want to save your time by not considering the things that people do for you, you will become bankrupt—bankrupt of quality people, quality ideas, and a quality company. Think back to when you felt like someone took you for granted. Maybe you made a career move because you didn't feel like you were properly recognized for the things you did. But if you invest some time "to ponder the nature of the contribution that other people make to your leadership,"[2] you will never go bankrupt.

Here is what you can focus on. Was there a successful project that they were a part of where you needed to recognize their efforts? Were they responsible for a certain task that they accomplished well? What do you appreciate about their character? Consider what they mean to you as a person as well as what they have helped you to accomplish.

In *The Leadership Challenge*, Barry Kouzes and James Posner found some interesting facts about leaders and appreciation. "When non-managers are polled regarding the skills their managers need in order to be more effective, at the top of the list is the ability to recognize and acknowledge the contributions of others."[3]

If you are having a difficult time discovering what to acknowledge, take the next step.

Take a walk

Take a walk to see what people are doing. Tom Peters called this management by walking around. In the *One Minute Manager*, Ken Blanchard said that we need to catch people doing things right. And according to Kouzes and Posner, "one of the most important results of being out and about as a leader is that you can personally observe people doing things right and then reward them either on the spot or at the next public meeting."[4]

Make a Scene... Through Letters

I was serving a new church start in the late nineties called Arise Church in Pinckney, Michigan. We held worship services in a local middle school gym and had to move a trailer full of equipment in and out

---

2.   Max De Pree, *Leadership Jazz* (New York: Dell Publishing, 1992), 114
3.   Jim Kouzes and Barry Posner, *Leadership Challenge* (San Francisco: Jossey-Bass Publishers, 1995)
4.   Kouzes and Posner, 289

every Sunday. There was a team of two or three guys who took on that responsibility every Sunday. When I would preach on Sunday mornings, I would write a 3X5 card of appreciation, thanking the moving team for all their hard work to make Sunday's worship a success. I wanted those people to know how much I appreciated their hard work, the kind of the work that got them to our office at 7a.m. in order for our worship to take place at 10:30 that morning. What they did was so important to the over-all success of providing a meaningful time on Sunday mornings that I didn't want them to feel taken for granted.

To be honest, I have probably forgotten some of the times when someone has told me how much he appreciated me for a job well done. But I have kept every letter of appreciation that I have received. I have a collection of letters from my last job, from my supervisor as well as my friends and colleagues. When you give someone a short letter, letting him know that you recognized their effort, they have something they can hold on to and read over in the future. Especially if you are someone important in their life, they will hold on to that piece of mail for a long time to come.

Make a Scene…Individually

Max DePree believes that "the most important part of a leader's job is acknowledging the efforts of other people and saying thank you."[5]

Again, it gets back to spending time on what is truly important in your leadership. When was the last time you told your husband that the meals he cooks were wonderful? When was the last time you told your wife that the lawn looked great? That doesn't happen in your home? Just a thought.

"I can't do anything without Deb Henning," said Lynn Wilde. Wilde works with actor Jeff Daniels at his Purple Rose Theater in Chelsea, Michigan and is president of the Pinckney Players. Henning

---

5.   De Pree, 111

has directed plays for Wilde and was the assistant director for Joseph and the Technicolor Dreamcoat in their community.

The people who work for Wilde return each time she produces a play because they feel appreciated by her. People have told her, "Your shows are so fun that we want to come to be a part of it." This came from one of her backstage crewmembers, not someone who gets to share the stage with other actors. I asked her why people come to work for her so readily. She replied, "Thank you, thank you, thank you." She writes them thank you notes. She tells them how much she appreciates them. "They do it because they know I need them. I grab their hand. I give them a hug. We laugh. I love to make people laugh."

Do the people around you know how much you need them? Stop reminding them of how much they need you. Do your customers know how much you appreciate the fact that they chose you over your competition?

Make a Scene…In Front of Their Friends

"Leaders find ways to shine the spotlight on the achievements of others rather than on their own accomplishments."[6]

Do you realize that you are in debt? You are indebted to the people around you who helped you become successful. When Isiah Thomas was inducted into basketball's Hall of Fame, he told the press that he would not have been there had he not been on a team of champions. He knew that he would not have received such a coveted award without the men he played with and the coach he played for on the Detroit Pistons.

Put the people around you in the spotlight, telling them in front of their peers how much you appreciate who they are and what they have done. Listen to that again. Make sure you not only appreciate what they have done, but also who they are.

---

6.   Kouzes and Posner, 204

Make a Scene…Often

The yearly review is helpful because it details how I am doing, but I would rather know what my boss thinks every week. Because life moves so quickly nowadays, we need to know that we are making a difference in our business. We need to know how we are making a difference as often as you can tell us.

I also want to know how I can improve. I'm not one to "just get by." I want to be the best I can be. Assume that about those around you. Tell them how they can improve, but sandwich your suggestions between comments of appreciation.

> ***Who needs to know that I appreciate them?***
> ***How can I show them today?***
> ***How can I show them off today?***

2

Do the people around you feel close to you?

o o o o o o o o o o o o o o o o o o o o o o o o o o o o o o o o o o o

"It's...important to build personal relationships to create the feeling of one company, one culture."

—*J. Carter Beese Jr, vice chairman of Alex Brown International*

I took a group of thirteen people with me to build a home for a family in Juarez, Mexico while I was on staff at Arise. This was my third trip down, and I was looking forward to this one with more anticipation than the others. I would have the opportunity to connect with someone I had a hard time connecting with for the two previous years.

We had the opportunities. We were next-door neighbors. We had similar interests. We worked with students together at our church. We had plenty of opportunities to work on our friendship, but for some reason we just didn't connect.

I pride myself on being a people-person. I don't do as well with tasks as I do with people. When I don't get something accomplished right away, it doesn't bother me as much as not connecting with someone.

How are you energized? Does it energize you to complete a task or talk to a friend? Connecting with others energizes me. When I don't connect, when I don't feel close to someone, it takes a lot of energy out of me because I feel like I should connect with everyone. Maybe it's an unrealistic expectation, but I want to be close with the people I associate with. It's not enough for me to get something accomplished with them. I also want to find out about them.

Mexico gave Barry and me a chance to connect like we didn't before. We were no longer neighbors. Michelle and I lived 45 minutes away. We were no longer partners in working with students because I got involved in a new church. We didn't have as many things to juggle between us. All we had to do was be friends and tackle a project of building a home together. I came home high from the trip, not only from building a home for a family, but also because Barry and I had fun working together, picking on kids together, and talking together.

Define the Feeling

When you feel close to people you feel like you connect with them. Michelle and I try to connect with each other everyday so that we maintain that feeling of closeness. It makes a difference in the level of our intimacy when we carve time out of our schedules for each other. Michelle and I get on each other's nerves when we ***don't*** spend enough time together. We started our relationship by doing everything together, and so we love spending as much time as possible together.

In the case of your business associates, you may not be best friends with them. When you are managing a plant, it would be impossible to maintain relationships with that many people. However, there are key personnel that you can connect with, teaching them and modeling for them the kind of business relationships they can have with others.

What better way is there to know your customer's present needs and expectations than developing a relationship with them? There is no better way to anticipate what those needs and expectations will be down the road than building customer intimacy.

How would you define closeness? Couples call it "being in love." Webster calls it being near in time, space, or relationship. When you are close with your friends, you might say you are "tight." When you are not close with someone, you feel like a wall has been built between you. The opposite of closeness is feeling faraway, distant, or removed.

Couples who no longer feel close say they are no longer in love with each other.

Walk in Their Shoes

We can get so caught up in "doing" that we forget to "be." "Being" must come before "doing." Life is a dance between being and doing. Sometimes we need to pull out all the stops to get something accomplished. At other times, we need to rest and just be. Besides, we are not called human-doers. We are called human beings.

When was the last time you spent some time to be alone with yourself? In this *i-exam*, I want us to focus on the relationships around us: parents, customers, friends, co-workers, spouse, children…It literally breaks my heart when I see a successful businessman who loses his wife. It breaks my heart to see a successful corporate woman gain the whole world but lose her family. Why are our businesses succeeding so admirably yet our families are struggling so horribly? It's time for our *i-exam*. When *i-exam*ine my closest relationships, what do I find?

i-exam

Who are my closest friends? (Could also be a family member)
What is it about this relationship that makes it close?
How well did/do my parents communicate with each other?
How well do I connect in my closest relationships?
How often do I get away with my spouse? Are we still dating?
Am I spending quality and quantity time with my children?
How well am I connecting with my business associates?
How well am I connecting with my clients?

Develop the Feeling

"Parents are prone to give their children everything except the one thing they need most. That is time."
—Emma K. Hulbert

We have a number of people that we need to stay connected with. Do you realize that you can have very fulfilling friendships? The problem with our level of communication is that we tend to learn all of our skills from home. I say this is a problem because so many homes have been broken by divorce, including mine. The way we learn how to develop the feeling of closeness with others usually comes through our personal experiences. What do we need to do to develop close ties to our families, customers, business associates and friends?

Get out of the office

"The spiritual journey that leaders must take, and inspire others to take, begins with ourselves but not necessarily by ourselves." [1]

Back in 1998, I approached the editor of our local paper on doing articles that would teach leadership lessons from the lives of leaders. The Express agreed and so I began my writing on leadership through the interviews that I conducted. The first person I interviewed was the leader of 530 staff members in the Pinckney Community School District. Mike Couchman, as the Superintendent of Schools, maintains a level of intimacy with the staff that he leads.

Mike sends a personal card for birthdays to his staff—his **whole** staff. He visits teachers after their summer break in order to find out how they are doing. In his spare time he carries cards around with him so that he can write them out. While we were talking he had a stack of

---

1. Lee G. Bolman and Terrence E. Deal, *Leading with Soul* (San Francisco: Jossey-Bass Publishers, 1995), 57

20 cards to deliver for that month. His staff love working for him because he takes personal interest in their lives. Obviously, Mike cannot be a close friend with all of them, but he can maintain some level of closeness so that they feel comfortable going to him if they have any concerns.

Mike leads from the heart. Everyone who has a birthday during that month has his or her name thrown in a basket. Whoever's name is picked, he does their job for the day, giving them the day off. He has taught classes, washed dishes, and cooked lunches. He also draws students' names for the month, taking them out for lunch with two people of their choosing.

Mike gets out of his office in order to spend time with those he leads. Some of us not only need to get out to spend time with co-workers or clients, but we also need to get out to spend time with our families. In your desire to make your business successful, don't sacrifice those who are closest to you.

Get out of your shell

What does your office represent to you? Does getting out of your office mean you have to get out of your shell? For a long time I felt more comfortable around other adults than I did around teens. It took me awhile to get "out of my office" when it came to relating with teens.

"What would I say?" I would ask myself. "What if I couldn't get them to open up to me?" I was really intimidated around them, thinking that the worst thing that could happen is to sit there in silence. "What if I couldn't relate?" Then I realized something about my attitude with them that was similar to my junior high days. Back in junior high I was so concerned with what others thought about me that it paralyzed me at times. By the time high school rolled around, I cared little about what others thought about me, and I had more friends than before.

That's when it dawned on me. I didn't have to make the kids like me. All I had to do was be myself. I stopped caring about what they thought of me. That is one way I had to get out of my office. I had to get out of my comfort zone so that I could…

Get into their lives

"The best minute I spend is the one I invest in people," said the *One Minute Manager*. Now that you are out of your office, or even out of your shell, it's time to get into the lives of those around you.

Find out what they are interested in. If you truly want to find out more about them, do what they do. Do they like to fish? Go fishing with them. Hopefully they like to golf, right? When you see your customers or your children in their natural environment, you will find out more about them than if you did what you were interested in. Tony Terlato of the Terlato Wine Group once told me you could tell a lot about a person after playing 18 holes of golf with them.

If you are in a place where you can get your front-line people into the lives of your customers, do it. "When you free your own people from transactional demands," said Dilip Saraf, senior consultant at QI International, "you free them up to build customer intimacy. And it's done through this intimate customer contact, face-to-face dialogue, or structured discovery—your own people sitting down with your own customer in a non-transactional setting, and asking, 'How is our marriage going?'"[2]

Get more out of them personally than what they can do for you corporately

Lynn Wilde works with actor Jeff Daniels at the Purple Rose Theater in Chelsea, Michigan. Lynn told me, "I like to treat people the way I want to be treated." This was the main reason Lynn got involved in the leadership of theater. She would see directors treat their crew very harshly. "Being an actress with other directors helped me to be a better

---

2.   J.P. Donlon, "CE Roundtable: Delighting the Customer," *Chief Executive*, June 1997, 57

director." She realized that there was more to the people around her than what they could do for her to pull off a production. She treated them with respect and developed a level of intimacy with them. This closeness with those she leads developed a very loyal following of volunteers who log in loads of hours and energy in order to pull off a quality production.

Grab your keys

First Key: *People skills*

"Person skills always precede professional skills." [3]

You may have the skills to close the deal, balance the books, or bus the table, but do you have the skills to make a friend? Leadership skills are sometimes lumped into two categories. The hard skills in leadership have to do with your technical know-how. You can build a web site, change the oil, or manage production. The soft skills in leadership have to do with your ability to connect with those around you. You can communicate with crowds or one-on-one. You know how to listen. You know that your body language says a lot to a person so you keep your eyes focused on them when you are talking. You know that it's not good to be pre-occupied mentally when you are trying to connect with them emotionally.

"Leadership is clearly a relationship predicated on personal involvement," Kouzes and Posner wrote in *Leadership Challenge*.[4]

But you cannot remain personally involved without people skills—the ability to get along with others. Kouzes and Posner sighted a study done by the California Department of Mental Health that states strongly how friends can be good medicine. "People with few close contacts were dying two to three times faster than those who regularly had friends to turn to."[5]

---

3.   De Pree, 221
4.   Kouzes and Posner, 298

The soft-skills in leadership are what the focus of this book is about. By focusing your attention on the feelings of those around you, you will be able to better develop those relationships to be meaningful for you and those you lead.

Second Key: *Personal commitment*

"If you want people to hang in there over the long term, if you want people to stay committed to the task, they have to stay committed to each other. Whether it's a dinner, a breakfast, an afternoon reception, or even just a meeting, gather people together to help cement social bonds."[6]

It's going to take a commitment of time and energy on your part to develop fulfilling relationships with your family and friends, clients and co-workers. The markets may fluctuate, but putting some emotional investment in the lives of those around you will always pay high dividends.

Third Key: *Pause*

"I think the ability to stop is an important trait of leaders." [7]

One of my jobs in the early nineties took me into some very large plants in North Carolina. To go from one end to another took a long time. It was great exercise, but I would have loved another form of transportation to get me around those facilities. A bike or a golf cart would have saved a lot of time and money, right? Maybe not.

Supervisors under Max Depree's leadership were not allowed to ride bikes at the Herman Miller plant. "You can't tap a person going by on a bicycle on the shoulder and say, 'Could I talk to you a minute?'" For

---

5. Kouzes and Posner, 302
6. Kouzes and Posner, 265
7. De Pree, 225

Depree, leaders had to have the ability to stop—"to ask and answer questions, to be patient, to listen to problems."

You are known as a go-getter. You would not have gotten to the place you are at today without making things happen. However, you not only need the ability to go, you also need the ability to stop. Take a look around you. Be available for the people around you. A great suggestion came through Kouzes and Posner's study:

"The most genuine way to demonstrate that you care and are concerned about other people as human beings is to spend time with them, so schedule some time daily just to get acquainted with others. This time shouldn't be yet another business meeting; instead, plan on unstructured time to joke and kid and learn more about each other as parents, athletes, musicians, artists, or volunteers."[8]

Where is there a wall in a relationship I'm in?
How can I open the door in that relationship today?
Am I connecting with my co-workers and clients?
How about my friends and family?

---

8.   Kouzes and Posner, 171–172

3

Do the people around you feel competent?

o o o o o o o o o o o o o o o o o o o o o o o o o o o o o o o
"You don't earn a living. You learn a living."

—*John Guffey Jr., Chairman and CEO*
of Coltec Industries

Eighteen leaders were assembled for *Chief Executive's* roundtable to discuss the education of their employees. J.P Donlon, editor-in-chief of *Chief Executive* noted, "If anything keeps CEOs up at night, it's ensuring that their companies will have the right people with the right skills necessary to be competitive." Sighting a Pricewaterhouse Coopers survey, Donlon went on to say "the percentage of business chiefs that say the lack of skilled workers is the No. 1 barrier to growth increased from 30 percent in 1993 to 65 percent in 1997." The leaders on the roundtable noted that employee education and training reduced the rate of turnover.[1]

Define the feeling

Being competent is feeling like you know what you are doing. When I was looking for a job in February of 2000, I looked at a lot of different

---

1.   J.P. Donlon, "CE Roundtable: Educated Employees," *Chief Executive*, April 1999, 68

companies that took just as many different skills. After trying to apply for a sales position, I came to realize that I wasn't a salesperson. I was a writer and communicator. I had to find a job where I could use the skills that I felt competent in. Trying to be something I'm not did not feel that great. In fact, it felt very uncomfortable. I had to do something that I enjoyed doing and was good at.

That's when a job with the *Insider Business Journal* opened up. I saw the ad in the paper and wondered if I could be a business writer. My passion is leadership. I love leading. I love hanging out with other leaders and learning from their lives. When you feel competent in your line of work, when you know what you are doing and can do a quality job in doing it, you will be more fulfilled in life.

Walk in their shoes.

At one of my previous jobs, I had to do some things I was neither good at nor enjoyed. When you are in a job like that, 20 hours seems like 40. When you are in a job that you love and are good at, 40 hours seems like 20. When you are competent you are energized. When there is room for growth and your company believes in you and puts money behind your personal and professional development, you want to stay with them. In the words of Allied Signal's Fred Poses, "you've got to give them a reason to stay with your company. You can make your company a great place to be by creating an environment where people continue to learn."[2]

i-exam

When have I felt competent?
What did people say I was good at growing up? What about now?
What strengths have people noticed about me?
Did anyone in my family or organization help me feel that way?

---

2.   Ibid., 72

What did they do to bring me to some level of competence?
When have I felt incompetent?

Develop the feeling

It's fine to have a company mission statement and a strategy to reach short and long-range goals. But "unless you give people the skills and tools to do something about achieving the high expectations we're all setting, you're just going to have frustrated employees."[3]

Allied Signal is a New Jersey-based manufacturer of aerospace and automotive products that believes in making its people feel competent. They want to have 40 hours of professional development per year for every person in their company, development that is tailored to each individual.

Cross Training

HarperCollins Publishers has an in-house course that teaches people about all aspects of the publishing industry. "We put our marketers in with our editors," said President and CEO, Jane Friedman, "and our IT people in with our salespeople and encourage the young people in various areas of the business to learn all about publishing."[4]

This gives everyone not only a better understanding of your industry as a whole, but it also helps them move into another area of your business. A *Time Magazine* article even went so far as to suggest that companies should train their people for their next job. Hopefully that next job is in your company.

Some in Generation X grew up watching their parents work their lives away only to be fired in an effort to boost profits. We see job security very differently because of this.

"To a Gen X-er, job security means having the kind of marketable skills that make you attractive to the next company or enable you to

---

3.   Ibid., 73. Comments by Frederic M. Poses, President and CEO of Allied Signal.
4.   Ibid., 76

start your own business," said Bruce Tulgan, co-founder of Rainmaker Thinking, an employee consulting firm that specializes in Gen X issues. "It has nothing to do with earning a gold watch after 25 years on the job."

"From talking to our employees I know that Gen X-ers want portable skills," says Carolyn Bell, who owns 48 franchised Supercuts hair salons in Florida and Texas with her husband Doug. Carolyn was a Supercuts hairstylist 12 years ago. "They want to know that whatever they learn from us can travel with them to the next job."

In an effort to make her employees feel competent, Carolyn visits with her stores and arranges for industry professionals to speak to the staff. "We'll do seminars on new hair products, new styling techniques or even what it's like to own your own salon," she says. "At first I was a little fearful about bringing that last part up. I didn't want to send the message that we were pushing anyone out the door."

"Training folks for the next job boosts loyalty," noted columnist Susan Caminiti. "In the past 18 months, turnover in the Bells' salons has dropped nearly half from 75% to 45%."[5] It pays to focus your attention on your co-worker's competence.

Strength Training

What are the skills they need to do their job the best? Whether I am writing or speaking, I ask people how I can improve. I don't have formal training in writing. When I began at *The Express*, I asked Heather Schulz to teach me as I wrote for her. When I moved on to the *Insider Business Journal*, Cal Stone helped me hone my skills as a business writer. When I started writing for *Vineyard & Winery Management*, Graham Parnell had to teach me what it took to write in the wine industry. Depending on the size of your organization, you don't have to have a full-blown training program. You can bring your people

---

5.   Susan Caminiti, "Managing: Young And Restless. Dealing with Generation X...," *Your Company*, February 1, 1998, 36+.

together on a monthly basis to sharpen their skills. You can mentor them one-on-one.

Seventeen-year waitress, Madeleine Albert, started conducting restaurant-service workshops in 1992. In 1995, she began working for Whole Foods Market, which is one of the largest chains of natural-foods supermarkets in the United States with 105 stores. At Whole Foods, Albert started the company's first service-specific training program.

"The first thing that I ask managers who want to improve the service at their companies is 'what's it like to work for you? Do your employees *feel* appreciated and respected?'"

Be Specific

Tell them specifically what you expect of them as you train them. Albert continued, "The average work environment isn't terrible; it's average. And consequently, so is service. To get people to deliver exceptional customer service, you have to be specific about what that means. Too many managers just tell their employees to 'be friendly.' But friendliness alone is not enough: A friendly ticket agent who loses my reservation and causes me to miss my flight is just going to leave me frustrated.

"Employees need to understand, in detail, what makes delighted customers 'delighted' and how to re-create that. At the same time, it's important to leave room for employees to use their own personality and their own ideas—to do whatever it takes to make customers happy. That means thinking of solutions, rather than falling back on policies.

"Our customers see our people not just as employees but also as experts in particular areas of the food industry. So we need to make sure that we give employees the information that they need to do their jobs. For example, our produce comes from all over the world, and some of it is very unusual. We make sure that team members can tell customers where and how various types of produce were grown, what they taste like, and how to prepare them.

"We know that it benefits our customers to get that kind of great service. But we also want members of our staff to understand how it benefits them to offer such service. Beginning on day one of training, team members understand that the difference between service and servitude lies in the dignity that only they can bring to the position. They know that the more they pay attention to the details of their job, the more rewarding it will be. That's the bottom line: All of us want to go home each night *feeling* proud of the way that we spent our time that day."[6]

Don't be surprised

> *"Where parents do too much for their children,*
> *the children will not do much for themselves."*
> *—Elbert Hubbard*

Part of the problem we have in making people feel competent is doing too much for them. We should not be surprised when people begin to perform on a higher level.

I feel like my daughter, Christina, is growing every day. She obviously is, but I feel like I see something new in her every day. She seemed mature even at the age of four.

An act as simple as programming the microwave shouldn't surprise me. But we were having lunch together when she was going to warm up some chicken noodle soup. I got up to help her, but was interrupted in my action.

"Stay there, Daddy. I'll do it," she said. "Mommy, now what do I do?" From there Michelle told her how to warm up her own lunch and she did it.

---

6.   McCauley, pp 93.

When we give people the tools they need to succeed, we should not be surprised at how fast they pick things up. Part of helping the people around us feel competent is letting them go. Let them go and let them grow.

> ***Everyone needs to grow in their level of competence.***
> ***What can I do today that will help those around me***
> ***become more competent, and more confident?***

4

Do the people around you feel like they have a sense of direction?

○ ○

"Realize that people are not only concerned about the direction of their company, but even more importantly, the direction of their lives."

—*John E. Aho*

Time Magazine columnist, Susan Caminiti, told a story about a woman in her first assignment in the marketing department of a major New York insurer. Katie Hunt, a young woman of 23, was disillusioned by a job that consisted of data entry work that made her job boring and unrewarding. Feeling lost, Hunt asked her marketing manager for something more challenging. She wanted to do something more than just enter numbers into a computer. All she got from her boss was a brush off. "I'll think about it," her boss said. Hunt quit six months later.

Hunt landed a job, making less money but gaining a sense of direction. As an assistant to the owner of a small creative design firm, she realized that "everyone gets to participate. I'm learning production, marketing, public relations. There's really no part of this business I can't learn about if I want to." Having a sense of direction has a lot to do with feeling competent in your career. Hunt was given the opportunity to learn competencies in other areas of her company, which added to her sense of direction in life.

Caminiti asked a great question. "What grand attractions do entrepreneurial firms have an exclusive on? The sort of culture that allows Generation X-ers—the 45 million men and women born between 1965 and 1977—to have the two things they value most: involvement with many parts of the business and interaction with the decision makers with a minimum of red tape."[1]

Define the feeling

Lynn Wilde told me, "You have to know what you're doing and where you're going." Why not just go with the punches and fly by the seat of your pants? Isn't it good to maintain some flex-ability? Flex-ability is fine, but it has to be balanced with a sense of direction.

We were at a friend's log home lodge in upper Michigan for Memorial weekend one fall. From I-75 we took a lot of side roads to get there. I am always trying to find new ways to go somewhere, so I looked at a map to see if we could go exploring on our way home. Our goal was to get home. That goal could not change because I had to be at work the next day. But to get home, we had the flex-ability to take the freeway or go another route that we had never been on before. Having some, and I do say some, flex-ability on the road of life is necessary. But if all you have is fluctuation, you won't get anywhere and the people around you will be lost.

There is a difference between Michelle and me when it comes to trip taking. She has to know exactly where we are going by looking at a map. My driving drives her crazy anyway. I don't want to compound the problem by not providing her with a sense of direction. She has to know where we are going.

The people we lead need to know where we are going. People get lost without a sense of direction. Lynn Wilde found that when she

---

1.   Caminiti, 36+

didn't provide her cast and crew with some sense of direction, they didn't know where they were going. Wilde never has the whole cast on the set at the same time. She works certain acts on certain nights, and so all they see is their part. It could be confusing for her crew if they don't know where she is going.

It may be confusing to your crew when they only see the part that they play and don't see the over-all direction of the organization. Show them where they are on the map of life, so they know how their contributions make a difference in the trip that your organization is taking. And also realize that people are not only concerned about the direction of their company, but even more importantly, the direction of their lives.

Walk in their shoes

1998 and 1999 were probably the toughest on me personally. Among the many things I was dealing with, I lacked direction. Being lost in a car is not that big a deal for me. Being lost in life is tough. I couldn't seem to make decisions with any kind of certainty. I was second-guessing myself. When *i-exam*ined the road of my life, I knew that I was lost. I had the sick feeling in my stomach that I wasn't where I needed to be. Was I always that lost?

All throughout 1997 I knew where I was going. I was coming back home to Michigan after graduation to be Leadership Developer for Arise Church. I got lost personally when we got lost as an organization. We didn't have a sense of direction, and we weren't sure if my position would continue to be funded. When the organization you lead has lost its direction, whether that's a city, a company, a family or a church, the people in that organization feel lost as well.

i-exam

When have I lacked direction in my life? How did that feel?

Have I ever been in an organization where I felt like they had no idea what they were doing? What did that feel like?

What has it been like to be a part of an organization that has a vision for the future?

Have I ever followed someone who changed directions a lot? What was that like?

What is it like for others to follow me? Do they know where I'm going?

Develop the feeling: *Developing Direction*

Enlist

Part of my problem is that I didn't feel like I had any say in the direction of our organization. But then Pastor Doug McMunn brought the leaders of our church together to dream. Our time together led us to discover a new territory, chart a new course, and begin a journey where we knew where we were going. Doug realized that he was not the only person with a vision. He let us in on the plan. A large part of feeling like you have direction is feeling like you have a say in the direction of your organization. You have a say in the vision.

Steve Camden is the fictional lost executive in Lee Bolman and Terrence Deal's book, *Leading with Soul.* Steve was told by the founder of the company to go see Maria, a wise woman who lived up in the mountains. John, in realizing that Steve was lost, sent him to someone who had helped him find a sense of direction.

In his first meeting with Maria, he told her how he had tried everything. New time management strategies. Mission statements. Strategic planning. Re-engineering. Hired consultants. Read magazines. After all he attempted, he still felt lost. He told her he needed a vision, but that it was hard for him to see beyond the next week. He told her he was lost.

After a number of trips driving up the mountain to gain some sense of direction, Steve realized a pretty profound, yet simple, truth. Steve had just brought his company together for their anniversary to remember their past, celebrate their present, and look to their future. During a video presentation, it dawned on him.

"We opened with another video," Steve told Maria over the phone. "Young people from around the world. Employees and customers. Talking about their dreams—what they hoped we'd become. Powerful, eloquent, inspired stuff. Reminded me how crazy it was to think of myself as the sole source of vision."[2]

As you try to gain a sense of direction for yourself as well as the people around you, remember that you are not the sole source of vision. There are other people looking at the road map of life who may find a better route to take in order to get to your destination. Enlisting the help of others will help you find a greater sense of direction than just taking them on a journey you want to take.

The authors of *Built to Last* say that creating a BHAG (big, hairy, audacious goal) as a team creates a clear and compelling vision for the future and "serves as a unifying focal point of effort—often creating immense team spirit. It has a clear finish line, so the organization can know when it has achieved the goal; people like to shoot for finish lines."[3]

Encourage

Once you have enlisted your Core Leadership, you need to encourage them on the way. Michelle and I created a new vision for our lives. We still wanted to make a difference in our community through our faith, but we wanted to do so by working outside of the ministry. We didn't want to ask for a salary as the leader of a new church. This led us to

---

2.   Bolman and Deal, 136

3.   James C. Collins and Jerry I. Porras, *Built to Last* (New York: HarperBusiness, 1997), 94

decide between a couple different jobs. Do I take a job that is higher paying as a computer trainer, or do I take a lower paying job as a staff writer? We chose the writing position because this is what I love. After a couple weeks of working at the *Insider Business Journal*, I told Cal that I felt high because I was doing what I loved—writing business news for business leaders.

Since I was out of work for a month, it created a burden on us financially. That burden made Michelle question whether our decision was the right one. I had to be her cheerleader, encouraging her to see what was ahead so that we could get through the things that held us back.

> *"Cheerleading—you won't find the word cheermanaging in the dictionary—is a crucial dimension of personal-best leadership experiences."*
> *—Kouzes and Posner*

You have to be the cheerleader for your organization and for your family. Once you have established the vision, once you have started with the end, you now have to encourage the people around you as you go. There is a lot of excitement when you discover a new direction and begin working to get there, but the honeymoon ends quickly and you realize there are still bumps in the road as you drive towards the new direction.

> *"Always have something to shoot for."*
> *—Paul Galvin, Founder of Motorola*

Entrust

Many of our feelings are intertwined. In order to make the people around you feel like they have a sense of direction, you have to make them feel like you trust them by giving them the freedom to move in that direction. You can't be hovering over their back, second-guessing every move they make.

David Packard said you have to "provide a well-defined objective, give the person as much freedom as possible in working toward that objective, and finally, provide motivation by seeing that the contribution of the individual is recognized throughout the organization."

After the objective has been defined, we as leaders need to give the people around us as much freedom as possible in working toward the new vision.

Is there someone who feels lost?
What can I do today that would help them gain a sense of direction?

5

Do the people around you feel free?

o o o o o o o o o o o o o o o o o o o o o o o o o o o o o o o o o
"People need to feel free enough to be naturally who they are."

—*Max DePree*

We don't deal with failure very well. In fact, everything we read about has to do with being a success. Failure for some of us means death. Failure is dark. Failure ends. However, there are leaders and businesses that are not afraid of failure. The businesses that, in the words of John Maxwell, fail forward are the ones that allow their people the freedom to experiment, freedom to be themselves, and the freedom to try out new ideas.

You can fail without being a failure.

William McKnight, after seeing the necessity of building 3M on more people than just himself, had the vision to make sure his company would continuously improve. It wasn't enough to have one person coming up with new ideas. He wanted his whole company to be infused with dreamers, employees who exercised their individual initiative.

People throughout 3M's history could be heard saying, "Listen to anyone with an original idea, no matter how absurd it might sound at first…Encourage; don't nitpick. Let people run with an idea…Hire good people, and leave them alone…If you put fences around people, you get sheep. Give people the room they need…Encourage experimental doodling…Give it a try—and quick!"[1]

From the company's early days, people felt free to experiment, free to make mistakes, and free to bring something new into the market. Bill Hewlett commented about 3M, saying, "You never know what they're going to come up with next. The beauty of it is that *they* probably don't know what they're going to come up with next, either. But even though you can never predict what exactly the company will do, you know that it will continue to be successful."[2]

Define the feeling

To be free means you are not imprisoned. The door is open. The chains are off. When you are free, you are not under any obligations. You are at liberty to do what you want when you want. You feel liberated, unfastened, emancipated, unconfined, unobstructed, unrestricted.

You don't want your freedom to launch into carelessness or looseness, however. Seasoned quarterbacks have the freedom to change the plays on the line of scrimmage, but they still have to follow the rules of the game. There are guidelines. They aren't totally free. But since they know the game plan, and since they know the plays they could call, they have the freedom to make the calls if they think another play would be more effective.

"Employees need to understand, in detail, what makes delighted customers 'delighted' and how to re-create that," said Madeleine Albert of Whole Foods. "At the same time, it's important to leave room for employees to use their own personality and their own ideas—to do whatever it takes to make customers happy. That means thinking of solutions, rather than falling back on policies."[3]

---

1.   Collins and Porras, 152
2.   Collins and Porras, 150
3.   McCauley, pp 93

Walk in their shoes

Parenting is a process of giving your children incremental freedoms. Whether it's programming the microwave, teaching them how to swim, or helping them learn on the computer.

Robert Wolgemuth wrote a book that deeply impacted my relationship with my girls, Christina, Sierra and Rebecca. In his book, *She Calls Me Daddy,* Wolgemuth says "if you overprotect, your daughter will develop an unhealthy, long-term dependence on you. Then she won't learn to make her own good decisions. She can't renew a driver's license or fill out an insurance form. She won't drive a two-hour trip on her own. Don't let this happen. Give your daughter a taste of independence when she's small."

Michelle worked at the Family Fitness Factory in Brighton, Michigan, teaching parent-tot swim lessons. It was structured to teach the parents to teach their children swimming. About once a week I would come in on one of her classes, and each week both of the girls grew in their ability to swim.

It was scary letting Christy swim to me for the first time. It wasn't like having her walk to me when she was younger. The worst that would happen then is that she would fall on her well padded behind. She could drown if I gave her too much freedom. But soon, Christy was even doing the back float, and could stay on her back for minutes at a time if she wanted to. It illustrated the difficulty of giving too much freedom too early, or not enough freedom too late.

i-exam

When have I felt micromanaged?
When have I felt confined or restricted?
What could I accomplish if I had all the resources I needed?
What happened when I was given the freedom to accomplish the goals in my way?

What did it feel like when I failed at something? What did I learn from failure?

Do I find myself looking over people's shoulders or staying out of their face?

Develop the feeling

Learn to dance

"Recognize the difficulty of holding people accountable while giving them space to make mistakes."
—Max Depree

This feeling is difficult to develop. Just like all the feelings, it takes a level of intimacy with those you are working with. Push them too hard too fast, they will burn out quickly. Push them too little too late, they will be bored out of their mind. Understand where they are at in their development, and let them be honest with you. Ask them what they need. Do they need more support from you, or do they need you to back off?

Let them step on your foot

"My mom and dad were stern at times," said Darrell Seering, a friend of mine from Michigan, "but they let me think and make decisions on my own. When I made the wrong decisions, we would discuss them. In Scouts and with my own kids, I let them do it on their own. The way young people grow is to give them latitude and then to assist them in making decisions. This helps them realize they must live by the consequences of their decisions."

Let them lead

Paul Galvin at Motorola "encouraged dissent, discussion, and disagreement, and gave individuals the latitude to show what they could do largely on their own."[4] And William McKnight knew that "mistakes will be made (by giving people the freedom and encouragement to act autonomously), but...the mistakes he or she makes are not as serious in the long run as the mistakes management will make if it is dictatorial and undertakes to tell those under its authority exactly how they must do their job. Management that is destructively critical when mistakes are made kills initiative and it's essential that we have many people with initiative if we are to continue to grow."[5]

As you're dancing, don't hold on too tightly

One of my favorite bands growing up was Triumph. The song, *Hold On Loosely*, speaks to this concept of helping others feel free. "Hold on loosely, but don't let go. If you cling too tightly, you're gonna loose control."

> *Is there anyone around me who needs some coaching?*
> *Are there people around me who I need to let go of?*

---

4.   Collins and Porras, 38
5.   *Our Story So Far* (St. Paul: 3M Company, 1977), 12

6

Do people feel good about themselves when they are around you?

o o o o o o o o o o o o o o o o o o o o o o o o o o o o o o

"People who feel good about themselves produce good results."

—*Blanchard & Johnson*

Do the people around you feel good about themselves? Have you ever been around a person that made you second-guess what you said and did? If people produce good results when they feel good about themselves, it should be our job to build them up.

John Maxwell says, "Hurting people hurt people." The opposite is also true. Healthy people bring healing. Hurting people that have been healed are the best healers. Hurting people that have been healed can best identify with other hurting people that need healing. The people who give simple answers to life's not-so-simple problems are usually the ones who have never gone through life's not-so-simple problems.

Self-esteem. What thoughts do you have about yourself? How do people think about themselves when they are around you? If you esteem yourself positively, you value who you are. You respect who you are. You take pride in who you are and what you accomplish.

Dan Reiland defines charisma as "making others feel good about themselves." We have traditionally looked at charisma as being attractive. If you are charismatic, you attract people. What Reiland is saying about charisma is that it has more to do with how the other person feels when around you than it does about your magnetism. What attracts people to you is that you make them feel good about themselves.

Define the feeling

> *"Only a person who has faith in himself is able to be faithful to others."*
> —*Erich Fromm*

What depreciates the value of a home? Cracked paint, non-working fixtures and appliances, a house next door in disrepair. A home that is connected to city water and sewage systems sells higher than a home with a well and septic tank. When my dad was trying to sell his home, he power-washed the deck, had the exterior repainted, cleaned the gutters, repaired a damaged interior wall…all in an effort to make the home look even better. He knew that any of those things would depreciate the value of the home.

There are many people around us that have weathered so much pain that their value has depreciated. They don't look at themselves very highly. We have the opportunity as leaders to help people's lives appreciate in value.

Erich Fromm's statement above shows us that when I have faith in myself, I am more able to be faithful to others. Jesus said, love others as I would love myself. That would be a problem for the people around me if I don't love myself that much. Feeling good about myself means that I love who I am. I admire the person that I am becoming. I esteem myself highly, but not too highly. I can be honest about my weaknesses but I can also be proud of my strengths. We can help the people around us feel that way about themselves.

Walk in their shoes

"Love your neighbor as you love yourself."
—Jesus

On Father's Day 1999 we got together as a family at the annual family golf outing at Lakelands Golf & Country Club. We played nine holes together, competing with other families the same size. This would be the last Father's Day I would have with my dad.

On Wednesday night of that week, I received a phone call from my brother, Andrew. He told me that I needed to call dad. I called and received the news. Dad had been diagnosed with leukemia. After a short month and a half fight, dad passed away on August 5.

A man who made us feel good about ourselves

All throughout his stay in the hospital, during the nights that I would stay with him in his room, and the long days of waiting and praying, dad would tell me, "I love you." Out of the blue during the middle of the night, when it was too uncomfortable for him to sleep, I would hear, "I love you, hon."

We talked a lot during those days and nights of fighting for him and fighting the disease with him. We talked about my grandparents and how they raised him. Whether grandpa was easy on him or tough, it was all in an effort to help dad be the best he could be. I began to see the ways that dad raised me, whether he was easy on me or tough, he did it in an effort to make me feel good about myself.

After we lost him, I wanted his memorial service to be special. As word got out to family, friends, and business associates, we realized that the church he went to would not hold the people who wanted to come. Business associates came from as far as Germany. We reserved another church in the area and were able to hold a wonderful memorial service for him.

The church held 500 people. The sanctuary was full, with many in the cry room and standing in back. I had read Reiland's definition of charisma some time before then, but that day I realized what it meant. I saw it embodied in my dad. What made dad magnetic was that he was charismatic. Dad made others feel good about themselves.

i-exam

What are my strengths? List them out.
What are the areas I can improve in?
Who made me feel the best about myself?
What did they do to make me feel that way?
How did they treat me?
What did they say to me?

Develop the feeling

"Friendship with oneself is all-important, because without it one cannot be friends with anyone else in the world."
—Eleanor Roosevelt

You have to have it to give it

"I couldn't pick out one certain story," Andrew told me about dad, "because it wasn't something he tried to do here and there. It was all the time. His smile of approval, and just the genuine way he was. You knew he wasn't fake at all. Dad always made me have a good feeling just by the way he was. He was a father and he loved that. He spent as much time with his kids as he could, and enjoyed every second of it." There is a key point here. Be honest, truthful, and have a genuine spirit, and it will shine through. You can always make someone's day with a smile when they know it comes from the heart. My father felt that way, and I thank God for heredity!

You have to have it to say it

"Sticks and stones may break my bones but names will never hurt me."
Since when? I have dealt with physical pain much better than I have emotional pain. John Grenfell, a long-time friend and pastor, told me that I
should believe about ten percent of what people tell me. If the comments
are negative, I won't let them go to my heart. If they are positive, I won't
let them go to my head. That's still difficult to do.

When you live in a community of apartments, you can hear when
someone yells at their children, calling them stupid or something worse.
If you call someone stupid long enough, they're going to believe it. However, the reverse is also true. If you tell someone how bright she is long
enough, she will believe it.

A friend of mine, Todd Borek, was told by his mom: "Son, be a leader,
not a follower."

Ever since my conversation with Todd, I have told my girls that same
thing. I ask them everyday, "Do you know how smart you are? Do you
know that you are beautiful?" They reply confidently, "Yes." They will
even ask me, "I'm beautiful aren't I?" or "Aren't you proud of me,
Daddy?" I'll reply confidently, "Yes you are." I don't want them to ever
feel like they are not bright or beautiful. If I have anything to say about it,
they won't struggle with their self-esteem.

Gene Nemerowicz and Eugene Rosi wrote a book called, *Education
for Leadership and Social Responsibility.* In the book they concluded,
"Many parents and teachers are not nurturing children's leadership
skills. Only 36 percent of the children recalled being told by anyone that
they would make a good leader.... Of the children who said they did not
aspire to reach a position of leadership, 90 percent never had been told
they would make a good leader."

The problem that these two educators see is that "many schools and
parents are nurturing the values associated with leadership, but they're
not using the right words to accompany their lessons." Don't let that
slide by you. They are helping to nurture the qualities of leadership,

but **they are not using the right words**. "That's why it's crucial to actually use the words 'leader' and 'leadership.'"[1]

By believing in their potential

If you tell the people around you how much you believe in their potential, they will begin to believe in themselves. My dad believed in our potential.

My brother Jay told me, "When I was young, dad used the Socratic method of teaching with me, even though he probably had no idea he was doing so. The Socratic method is teaching by questioning. Once when we were in the car together, I started to ask him some questions about the tachometer. So he started to ask me some questions. For example, he asked what RPMs meant, and I answered. He followed that up with 'Why is it important for a car to drive at lower RPMs?' My answer of 'better fuel economy' was exactly what he was looking for.

"He led me to the answer by asking me questions," Jay remembered. "This taught me to do the same for myself later in life, but at that young age, it encouraged me. It made me feel like I knew the answers if I just tried hard enough. I did need to rely on someone to answer for me.

"Leaders at any stage of life can do the same thing," Jay encouraged. "They can lead the people around them by questioning a situation. They do not have to give the answer, but they can lead their team with questions. Doing this not only makes a teammate feel smarter, but it also eliminates a lot of second-guessing. If I ask a question, but I don't like the answer, I might challenge you on it. But if you lead me to the answer with questions, I will come to the answer on my own, and stick with it."

Who do I know that does not feel very good about himself?
What can I do today to make him realize his worth?

---

1. Kim Pryor, "Raising Little Leaders," *Kiwanis Magazine*, May 1999, 32

7

Do the people around you feel important to you?

○ ○
"Numbers don't mean anything...because it's people that count."

—*Will Rogers*

In an article in the *Minneapolis Star Tribune*, Dale Dauten tells about the owner of a manufacturing firm in Minnesota who wondered how he could improve working conditions in his company. Concerned that his employees might not open up to him the owner hired consultant Dennis Van Norman to interview the company's employees.

"Van Norman talked to every employee, looking for problems. The closest thing to a complaint was some comments about the difficulties of working the night shift and how the night employees hoped to one day change shifts. When the owner heard the results of the interviews, he zeroed in on the lone complaint and decided that he would reconfigure his plant, buy additional machinery and eliminate the night shift. That decision had to hurt the bottom line. After all, the company didn't have 'an employee problem' to solve and the decision meant buying extra equipment."[1]

What would make the leader of a company "zero in on one lone complaint?" The owner felt that every opinion was important, even if

---

1.   Dauten, pp 02D

it was just one opinion. Dauten wrote that there were no problems in the company, that nothing major needed correcting, but it didn't stop the owner from trying to improve working conditions. So he brought in an outside consultant in order to get some honest answers. One of those answers had to do with the difficulty of working the graveyard shift.

"Get over it," he could have said. "We're in the business to make money, and if that means keeping people on the late shift, fine. No one else is complaining." He could have taken that stance. But instead, he felt every person in his plant was important, and changed the way his company did business.

Define the feeling

As CEO of Resource Marketing in Columbus, Ohio, Nancy Kramer tells clients who say they want to own the customer, "you cannot own customers unless you earn them."

In order to earn the business of another company or customer, you have to show them that they are important to you and your business. She almost has to feel like she is your only customer. Her needs and expectations matter.

Feeling important means that you feel like you are number one in someone's life. You are unique. You are different. Everything about you matters. You have different goals, different ways of doing things. Who you are, what you say, what you believe…matters. You matter.

One of my favorite players on the Detroit Lions was Chris Spielman. Whenever I played football with friends, I got more excited if I could tackle the playmaker than making a touchdown. Spielman's intensity was awesome to watch. Commentators would remind the viewers where Spielman got his intensity for the game. He got himself worked-up by thinking the opposing team was trying to attack his daughters.

The love he had for football, though, came second to the love he has for his family. His wife, Stephanie was diagnosed with breast cancer.

Spielman made a decision that his wife mattered more than his football career.

"It was a very easy decision to make for me. I told her that I want to be the one to take her to treatments. I want to be the one to hold her hand. I want to be the one to be with my kids when she can't."

Spielman showed her how important she was by being there for her.

Walk in their shoes

Lunch @ Box Bar.

My parents were splitting up when I was entering my freshman year at Taylor University, and I placed all the blame for that on my dad. I didn't want to have anything to do with him. In fact, I didn't go to dad and Denise's wedding because I was so hurt. We continued as acquaintances for a year and a half.

Speed ahead to Spring Break my sophomore year. Dad wanted to take me out to lunch, so he picked me up and we headed to the Box Bar in downtown Plymouth, Michigan. He told me that he knew I had a lot on my mind, and that he needed to hear it.

"No matter how much you think it might hurt me," dad said, "I have to hear what you are going through." All the things I thought I would tell him in a heated argument came out in a calm conversation as we ate our bar burgers and potato wedges. Up until this point I had so much inside of me, I thought I would explode. Instead of opening the lid of my life quickly, he slowly opened me up and I was able to tell him everything that was on my mind.

That was really important in our healing, but he did something that became the turn-around in our relationship. I looked at my watch, noticed that we had been there for over an hour, and told dad that he needed to get back to work. I will never forget what he said and what he did for the rest of my life.

"I'll just call my secretary and tell her I'm playing hooky with my son." With that, we hung out for another hour and talked. Dad showed me that I was important to him. I got to return the love as we spent the last weeks together in his hospital room, showing him that he was very important to me as well.

i-exam

When have I felt important to someone?
What unique contributions or characteristics have others noticed about me?
What makes me different than others?
Have I ever been in a conversation with someone who wasn't there?
Have I ever been in a company that was concerned about my needs along with their own?
When have I been treated as an individual, and not just a number?

Develop the feeling

How do you make someone feel like they are number one when you literally have scores of people you work with, live with and play with? How can a company that employs thousands of people make one employee feel unique? How do you help the friends around you feel like they matter? What do you do to make one customer feel like he is the only one you have, even though you may have hundreds or thousands?

Realize your importance

Have you been made to feel important? You are. Your dreams, your goals, your ideas and ideals matter. The make-up of your gifts, your personality, and your experiences makes you unique, and if you do not believe that about yourself, you may not believe that about others. Hopefully you didn't cheat on the *i-exam*. You need to realize what it means to be important to others before you can help others realize it for themselves.

Believe in their importance

If you try to tell or show someone they matter before you believe it, you will not come across as sincere. You might, and I say might, get away with it with another adult, but don't even think of pulling that over on a teen. They can see right through you. Make sure you believe that she matters to your family, to your friendship, or to your organization.

Take some time to examine the beliefs you hold regarding the people around you. Do you believe that they can accomplish a task with the right resources? Do you believe that your high expectations of the people around you will be exceeded by them? Do you believe that their personal goals are just as important if not more important than their professional goals? How would your beliefs feed your actions?

Companies that don't believe a customer's comments are important will not guarantee a reply. Nancy Kramer believes that companies can show the importance of a customer by "doing what you say you'll do. We've found Web sites that say that someone will get back to you, but no one does. Or they say, 'Here's a place to ask us about our product'—and they have a disclaimer that reads, 'We cannot always answer every question that we receive.' There are more examples of sites that do service the wrong way than there are of sites that do it the right way."

Communicate their importance...

...by making it personal

"But there are also sites that absolutely win you over," Kramer continued. "For example, I love my interaction with Amazon.com. I have three children, and I've told the folks at Amazon that I'd like to get information about children's books. About a month ago, they sent me an email that was written in a way that *felt* personal, as if they were paying special attention just to me. I'm fond of a particular children's author, and the email said something like 'Because you've purchased several Rosemary Wells books in the past, we thought you'd like to know that she has a new book coming out.' And they told me all about the book. It was very friendly and nonintrusive. I *felt* that someone was watching out for me."[2]

That's what Kramer calls serving customers. It's "not just providing so-called customer service. It's remembering that at the root of the word 'service' is the word 'servant.' Those creating a commercial site online today must think of themselves as devoted servants of customers."

...by creating mutual goals

"When considering what you plan to accomplish, it's essential that you think and talk in terms of our goals. Your task as a leader is to help other people reach mutual goals, not your goals."[3] I have a vision for my life. Michelle has a vision for hers. Which one do we go with? If you answered both, you're right. Relationships split, no matter if they are professional or personal, because nobody wants to compromise. Whether you are establishing a set of company or family goals, you have to come at them together. Bringing others into the process of vision casting will not only bring about a greater vision, but it will also help them feel like they matter to you. Their lives, their ideas, their ideals matter to you.

...by doing little things that make a big difference

Executive Business Coach, Robert Sher, encourages leaders to "do little things to make your employees feel important." Sher gives an example of Herbert Kaufman, president and CEO for Burns & Wilcox Ltd., which is a national underwriting management and brokerage firm.

---

2.   McCauley, pp 93
3.   Kouzes and Posner, 170

"Ever since he founded his national firm, Mr. Kaufman has called each employee on his or her birthday to extend personal greetings. He also seems to remember the names of their family members—and what type of pets they have!"[4]

You don't have to go to great expense. The most memorable event in my friendship with my dad was a talk over lunch. The greatest things I receive from my children I get every day.

"Know how much I love you, Daddy?" Sierra asks. "This much," she says, spreading her arms wide.

Jim Mason, publisher of the Insider, popped into my office one day to tell me I did a great job on a story and that I should consider some other stories from that article.

Continue to think about the little things that can make a big difference. What makes the biggest difference is knowing what little things the people around you enjoy. Christina likes it when I lightly scratch her arms. Sierra enjoys big hugs. Michelle needs time to talk when I get home. A friend of mine likes to fish. A colleague loves music. Take some time to be with the people around you. Get to know their likes and dislikes. Show them how much they matter to you by doing little things for them.

...by changing the way you interact with them

Anthony Lye is President and CEO of NoWonder Inc., an online support marketplace on the Web. Lye has created an atmosphere in his company where customers and employees are made to feel important.

"Sometimes the only way to improve customer service is to change the model that you use," Lye encouraged. "Take technical support. The most frustrated customer has to be the one who's trying to fix a computer glitch. Why? Because it's service providers, rather than customers, who dictate the terms and the level of service. And that service

---

4.   Robert Sher, "Don't Forget to Thank Employees" *Corp! The Magazine of Successful Business*, March 2000, 75–76

is almost always both expensive and difficult to find. So the customers are unhappy—and, what's more, so are the service providers: They're not paid much, and they don't like the way that their work is structured. Most tech-support people leave their jobs after only 18 months."

In his case there were two big problems to work through. Customers were unhappy with the service they were receiving, and tech-support hated their jobs because they weren't paid well and didn't like how they were providing service.

"That's a no-win model," Lye continued. "We're trying to change that by offering tech support through an online network. We're like a big dating service, hooking up customers and providers. It's fast and personal. You get to know the name of your tech-service provider, and you don't have to go through the standard set of 20 questions every time you need help. You have a place to go 24 hours a day, 7 days a week; you can choose from among 5,000 experts—and find an answer to your problem. And the providers are happy too, because suddenly they've got freedom. They can choose when and how they'll work, and they have the opportunity to earn a lot of money."

When you show the people around you that they matter, that the time they spend trying to get a computer fixed is valuable, and that the employees you bring on ought to be treated with more respect, everyone wins. The result of showing this kind of attention to making people feel important has earned NoWonder a customer satisfaction rating of over 90 percent, and has helped them resolve over 50,000 questions a month, with over 70 percent of the problems solved in an hour or less.

Who doesn't feel very important in my life?
What can I do today to help them feel like they matter?

8

Do the people around you feel like they are part of a team?

o o o o o o o o o o o o o o o o o o o o o o o o o o o o o o o o o o
"No matter how much work you can do, no matter how engaging your personality may be, you will not advance far in business if you cannot work through others."

—*John Craig*

When you talk about the accomplishments of your family, your work area, or your company, do you talk in terms of "I did this" or "we did this?" There were a few people who didn't think that we could pull off our first mission trip to Mexico when we were only a two year old church.

We had to raise over $8000, recruit at least 15 people, and build a home. Granted, we weren't raising millions in venture capital for a new start-up company, but we were helping teens raise over $500 a piece. I may have been the one to spearhead the vision, but 18 other people made it possible. When we had a banquet a month after our trip, I gave gifts to those who worked behind the scenes to make it happen. From the start and to the end it was a team effort. Had I taken the credit for the success of the project, those who worked with me would have felt dejected instead of feeling injected with enthusiasm.

Carol Thybault was one of those behind the scenes people. She helped us launch the trip but she stayed behind. Yet she was so much a part of the team in the six months leading up to the trip and the month after, that kids were asking her, "Carol, do you remember when we had the windstorm on Thursday?" Carol had to remind them that she wasn't even there. That's what it means to feel like you are part of a team.

Define the feeling

"One man working with you is worth a dozen men working for you."
—*Herman M. Koelliker*

Feeling like you are a part of a team means you feel like you belong. When you belong, you have a sense of loyalty. You don't want to let the team down. You feel accepted unconditionally, with no strings attached. You're accepted, but you are held accountable. People care enough to confront. There is a sense of rapport among the group. To belong means to be a part of, to be related to or connected with. It means to be owned by or be in the possession of. When you are a part of a team you feel you are associated with something greater than yourself.

When interviewing leaders for *Leadership Challenge*, Kouzes and Posner developed a simple test to detect whether someone was on the road to becoming a leader. That test was the frequency of the use of the word we.[1]

Walk in their shoes

"Nobody works for me in this company. They work with me."
—*John Colone*

---

1.   Kouzes and Posner, 12

I do some things really well. I am a good communicator. I get along with people. I have some gifts as a musician. I see the big picture. I don't take things very seriously.

I do other things horribly. I don't see details. I am not good at accomplishing tasks. I tend to let my feelings rule when it comes to getting something done. "I'll do it when I feel like it," I regret, is sometimes my motto. I don't take things very seriously. No it's not a misprint. Sometimes your greatest strengths can also be your greatest weaknesses.

I have been successful when I have brought people around me who are gifted in the areas I am not. Leaders have to have enough confidence in themselves to bring around them people who are more gifted than they are. The only way you can live at your peak is to have others take the hike to the top with you.

I love what John Maxwell says about the phrase, "It's lonely at the top." He says that it's only lonely if you haven't brought people with you. By the way, being a leader means that people are following you.

i-exam

When I was growing up, when was I chosen to join a team?
When have I felt like I was a part of a team?
When did someone make sure I felt part of that team and what did they do to make me feel that way?
When have I felt left out?

Develop the feeling

See the need

> *"Don't use your people to build a great work;*
> *use your work to build a great people."*
> *—Jack Hyles*

"Leaders who see only a limited need for the gifts of followers limit themselves to their own talents."[2] You need to see what you need. Think of your organization as a body, and ask yourself what part you play. If you are the head, do you think you can survive on your own? No. You need the neck to turn you. If you think you're a finger, you still need the hand to point you in the right direction.

I'm an eye and a mouth. Some say I'm a big mouth. I see a vision and can articulate it, but I still need feet around me to go places and hands around me to get things accomplished. After you see where you are weak, you need to look for those strengths in other people. Bring people around you who will complete you instead of compete with you.

Let others lead

> *"In management's thinking, wages and job security always materialize as a major factor when in reality employees ranked a 'full appreciation for the work they do' and the 'feeling of being in on something' as the highest motivational factors."*
> *—William J. Ransom*

In *Leading With Soul*, Maria told Steve to "develop the courage to let others lead." Why does it take courage? Those who are not confident in who they are become fearful of bringing gifted people around them. They're intimidated by the strengths of others; fearful they may lose their job to one who is more gifted. But the more you push someone down, the further down you go. The more you lift people up, the higher you climb.

---

2.   De Pree, 14

Use the word "we."

"Practically everything we accomplish happens
through teamwork."[3]

When something goes wrong, who gets the blame? When something goes right, who takes the credit? One thing that has interested me about Presidential races is that they take the credit for the economy when it is strong, yet shy away from taking the blame when the economy is weak. Strong leaders take responsibility for the struggles and share the credit for the successes. When you talk about the accomplishments of your family, your organization, or your community, do you catch yourself saying "I" or "we?" Did "we" do this, or did "I" do it?

Who in my life does not feel like they belong?
What can I do today to make them feel like they are part of the
team?

---

3.   De Pree, 22

9

Do the people around you feel loved?

o o o o o o o o o o o o o o o o o o o o o o o o o o o o o o o

"If you're going to play together as a team, you've got to care for one another. You've got to love each other."

—*Vince Lombardi*

Yap Kim Wah, who is Senior Vice President of Marketing Services for Singapore Airlines stated, "the most important thing that you can do for customers is to make them *feel* cared for as individuals. That means doing the little things, looking for opportunities to provide extra customer care. It means making passengers *feel* as if everything you do were especially for them—how you serve a cup of tea, with just the right amount of sugar, or the way you empathize with a particular passenger's plight."

Wah went on to tell the story about an attendant who helped a passenger feel cared for.

"On a recent overseas flight, one of our attendants noticed a toddler who kept dropping his pacifier. Every time he dropped it, he would cry, and either his mother or another passenger would retrieve the pacifier, or the flight attendant would get it as she walked by. Finally, the attendant picked up the pacifier, attached it to a ribbon, and sewed it to the child's shirt. The child was happy, the mother was happy, and the passengers nearby gave the attendant a standing ovation for solving the problem so cleverly."[1]

Define the feeling

"Love...may be the best kept leadership secret of all."
—Kouzes & Posner[2]

I am using the terms **loved** and **cared for** interchangeably because I believe they are so intertwined. It's easy to talk in terms of making a friend or family member feel loved. It's more difficult to think of loving a customer or co-worker. When a flight attendant goes out of her way to personally make a customer feel cared for, they feel loved.

Out of all the feelings we could try to define, love would be the most difficult. Webster's definition says that love is an intense affection for another arising out of kinship or personal ties; a strong feeling of attraction resulting from sexual desire, and we don't want to go there when it comes to customers or co-workers. It can also mean enthusiasm or fondness. By the way, how did love ever come to define zero? Tennis anyone?

Instead of thinking of love in terms of a noun, I want to think of it in terms of a verb. When you feel loved and cared for, it's because someone has done something for you. Your parents are looking out for you. Your boss supports you by giving you the necessary resources.

One ancient writer had to put love in terms of about fifteen actions. Love is patient with those around you. Love is being kind to others. Love doesn't envy, wanting what someone else has. Love doesn't boast, saying, "look at me." Love is not arrogant. Being rude to others does not fit within the definition of love. Instead of insisting on its own way all the time, love allows the direction of a decision to be shared. Love is not irritable. Maybe it is until 10a.m., only after it has had three cups of coffee. Love doesn't resent someone for victories they have had in their lives. Love only celebrates when something is done right, not wrong. Love only celebrates when truth wins out over falsehood. You

---

1.   McCauley, pp 93
2.   Kouzes and Posner, 14

can lay a lot of burdens on love's shoulders because it bears all things. Love is the great believer—when all seems lost, love continues to hold out hope and says "bring it on" to anything that comes its way.[3]

"Love is loyalty," Vince Lombardy said. "Love is teamwork. Love respects the dignity of the individual. Heart power is the strength of your corporation."

Walk in their shoes

I was freelance writing for *The Express* and writing Leadership Lessons on leaders in my area. When my dad was diagnosed with leukemia, *The Express* sent him a card. I would visit dad probably five days out of the week and I just so happened to be there to open the card for him. I read the card to him, and showed him the picture of a mountain scene on it.

"I'll be darned," he said. "I was really having a rough day today, not wanting to get out of bed to go and take a walk." In order to keep his energy up, dad would take a walk around the hall. He was quarantined to a specific area because of the cleanliness of the air. Because of his engineering mind, he knew how many times it took to walk up and down the hall to make a mile.

"I then remembered my hike on Pike's Peak in the Rockies," dad continued. "There were times when I would be walking a path only a foot or two wide, with a 1,200 foot drop off to one side. I would stop, getting nervous about pressing on. But I would pray that God would get me through the next step, and He did. I gained enough strength to get through that narrow pass until I would reach the next one.

"I had one of those experiences today," he said. "I prayed for the strength, the mental strength it took to get out of bed and take my walk. God gave me the strength to get through this mountain pass, and then gave me the encouragement through that card."

---

3.   I put into my own words the words of an ancient Jewish leader, Saul of Tarsus, from 1 Corinthians chapter 13, verses 4 through 7 of any Bible.

Because the company I worked for cared enough to send a card, a card that touched dad in such a profound way, I felt loved by them. I wanted to work for them all the more.

After dad's memorial service, Michelle was looking through the cards we had received as we made our way back home.

"Johnny, listen to this." Michelle began to read the card. It was one of those cards that stuck out as better than the rest. The givers? *The Express*. The grateful receivers who felt loved by a simple act? My family.

i-exam

What does it mean for me to be loved by others?
How have the people around me—my family, friends, or co-workers—loved me?
How did it make me feel to have someone care for me like that?
Did it seem odd for someone at work to express appropriate care for me?
When have I not felt loved? How did it affect me?

Develop the feeling

> *"A leader's true love should be the people who do the work."*
> **—Max DePree**[4]

Take specific action

Love is a verb. In the book, *Leading With Soul*, Maria told Steve, "When people know that someone really cares, you can see it." Love is not only an action. Love is a specific action.

"Remember one thing, Steve. Everyone's different. A big part of love is caring enough to find out what really matters to others."[5]

---

4.   De Pree, 106

Caring for people means you are close enough to know what really matters to them. Dr. Gary Chapman directs marriage seminars throughout the country and wrote the best seller called *The Five Love Languages*. In his book, Chapman suggests that each of us speaks a primary language of love. Just like English is my first language, my first love language may be words of affirmation. That means I hear "I love you" when people pay me a compliment about who I am or what I have done. Michelle's primary love language is quality time. She hears "I love you" when we spend quality time together.[6]

What happens when I try to speak my primary language to her? She might appreciate it, but she may not understand that as "I love you" because I am not speaking her first language. I'm speaking in my own language. Michelle and I both studied Spanish in college, and she teaches English as a second language to others. We learned Spanish as a second language in order to communicate to others who don't speak English.

We have to do the same thing when it comes to loving others. We have to find out how they feel loved and cared for. What interests them? Do they like a certain kind of book? One of the greatest gifts I ever got from Michelle was the Star Wars Trilogy because she knew that the first movie held special meaning with me since that was the first movie dad and I ever went to see together.

This step is linked closely with feeling close to someone. You have to know them before you will know how to care for them in a way they will feel cared for.

Show and tell

According to researchers, there are three different types of assistance people need in order to cope with stress and adapt to change. They

---

5.   Bolman and Deal, 84–85
6.   Gary D. Chapman, *The Five Love Languages*, (Chicago: Northfield Publishing, 1992). Chapman and Dr. Ross Campbell also have a book out called *The Five Love Languages of Children*.

have also been "found to be necessary for enhancing the child's well-being. Children *feel* cared for and valued when parents are willing to spend time with them, which may alleviate some of their negative *feelings. Feeling* that they are part of a family network serves to reduce children's sense of isolation."[7]

When given this kind of support, children and adults alike feel loved, important, and feel like they are part of a team.

The first kind of support is **emotional support**, and is defined as "information parents provide to their children to indicate that they love and care for them." This kind of support includes what you may say to someone to let him know you care. Tell them what you love about them.

It was strange at first to tell my grandpa I loved him. We were not in the practice of doing it, and he may have thought it a bit odd as well. I mean, men don't usually tell other men "I love you," do they? Grandma and grandpa lived with us for a couple years, and every time I would go out my grandpa would tell me, "Be careful." Mom told me, "that's his way of saying, 'I love you.'" I'm glad that both my grandpa and dad have given me the gift of hearing those words.

The second is **esteem support**. "Esteem support is defined as information parents provide to their children to indicate that they value them." Let them know what you value about them. What makes them valuable to your family, friendship, or organization? Tell them. Write to them, letting them know what you prize about them. What about them could you not be without?

The third is **instrumental or problem-focused support**. This "is a combination of tangible aid and information." This is the kind of love

---

7.   Valery, Joan H.; O'Connor, Patricia; Jennings, Sybillyn, *The nature and amount of support college-age adolescents request and receive from parents.* Vol. 32, Adolescence, 06–22–1997, pp 323(15). They also site researchers Cobb, 1976; Cohen & Wills, 1985; Cutrona, 1990 and Moran & Eckenrode, 1991; Wills, Vacarro, & McNamara, 1992

that the flight attendant showed to the passenger and her child. She did something tangible to show them she cared about them as people.

One of my leadership lesson articles focused on the leadership of two parents, Darrell and Christine Seering. One of the ways that the Seerings showed their love in an instrumental way was to be present at their games. Even when Mark, Kim or Matt had something going on at the same time, one of them would be there.

"It expresses to them that they are loved and that you are interested in them and in what they do," Chris explained. "To me, it's depressing to be at a soccer game with 21 kids on the field with very little turn out from parents. We're putting other things ahead of our kids."

Darrell would find that many of the kids would look for him during a game. The students that were surveyed shared that their parents instrumentally showed their love by giving them support in ways that can be applied here. They received rides from their parents. It means a lot, even if you have to drop them off a couple blocks down the road. They asked for help in dealing with a problem with a friend. They received money for an activity. Parents listened to their feelings about a friend, a teacher, or another family member. They helped their children with schoolwork.

The research also suggested "a lack of support appears to make adolescents more cautious concerning interpersonal relationships. It may even lead them to *feel* that it is too risky to ask another for help. As a result they may perceive an absence of support, even when they have ample access to a concerned and potentially caring social network."

If you want to help the people around you feel loved and cared for, give them the support they need. Let your support fuel their desire to be confident concerning interpersonal relationships.

Who around me needs to be cared for?
What can I do today to make them feel loved?

10

Do the people around you feel motivated?

o o o o o o o o o o o o o o o o o o o o o o o o o o o o o o o o o o

"There are two great motivators in life. One is fear. The other is love. You can lead an organization by fear, but if you do, you will ensure that people won't perform up to their real capabilities."

—*Jan Carlson*

Mark A. Wallace is President and CEO of Texas Children's Hospital in Houston, Texas. As a leader, Wallace understands how motivating others in specific ways can help them overcome the greatest obstacles, including disease. When you are motivated, walls can be climbed, fences can be jumped, barriers can be broken.

"Finding ways to help sick children and their families *feel* better goes far beyond being a mere 'service,'" Wallace said. "It's part of the children' s recovery. After all, if children can *feel* the same level of nurturing and security that they *feel* at home, then they're going to get better a whole lot faster."

Wallace realized that if children had the opportunity to play and had access to their parents, it would help to distract them from their illness.

"We take kids to our playground, which has swings and sandboxes that are accessible to wheelchairs and gurneys," Wallace continued. An in-house radio station is also a part of keeping their hopes high. Children can get involved as disc jockeys, and those that can't go out of their rooms can listen in and still be involved in the contests. Not only are the children able to play a lot, "close contact with parents and families is critical for our patients. And often the children are so sick that their families don't want to leave the hospital anyway, not even to sleep in a nearby hotel. So we've created sleeping areas at the hospital where families can stay free of charge, and we're expanding those areas now."[1]

When you are facing a deadly disease, it is difficult to have much motivation to live. There were times when dad wasn't very motivated to take walks, or to do anything that would help him get better. He had the greatest attitude I knew of anyone, but there are still times when the strongest people need to lean on others to be motivated to live.

Define the feeling

"A leader—not a manager, a true leader—grasps the secret of employee motivation: Make it a job first-rate people truly want to do. This need not involve consultants or elaborate programs, just taking the time to figure out how employees' lives could be better."[2]

To motivate means that you are causing something or someone to act. If you are motivated, you have been prompted to act. You have been moved to do something. Something has stimulated your thinking and your actions. And the act of motivating others, in the words of Dwight Eisenhower, is the "art of getting people to do what you want them to do because they want to do it."

Walk in their shoes

Michelle is my greatest coach, and since she knows I hear "I love you" through words of affirmation, she lets me know how effective I am in

---

1.   McCauley, pp 93
2.   Dauten, pp 02D

what I do. Bill Crews, president of Golden-Gate Seminary, has a leadership library that is available to the students. That's when I got hooked on John Maxwell's leadership tape club. Michelle and I have been listening to John ever since 1997, just about every month.

As we were on a trip to see my brother and his wife, we were listening to one of John's Injoy Life Club tapes. Before the lesson, they announced John was coming to our area for a conference.

"Are you going?" Michelle asked. I told her I didn't think we could afford it. She told me to call them as soon as possible to make my reservations. "I know what you are going to do as a leader and I know how important this is." Having people around you who keep you up when so much can bring you down is imperative.

i-exam

What motivates me to action?
Who has been the strongest motivator in my life?
What did they do to encourage me to be better?
Has there been anyone in my life that took the wind out of my sails instead of breathing new life into me?
When have I coached myself to action?

Develop the feeling

Keep a plan to reform

In order to motivate we must first motivate ourselves. There are at least three habits that have to be unlearned in order for us to be motivated.

1. My habit of waiting for someone else to motivate me.

What I have personally learned through John Maxwell's leadership teaching is that I cannot develop others until I develop myself. I must develop the leader within me as I am developing the leaders around me. The only way I can teach others how to motivate themselves is for me to be my greatest coach. You cannot lead people to a place that you have never been.

2. My habit of waiting until I feel like it.

Is there an area in your life where you need to be motivated? I would start with physical exercise, but everyone is so effective in that area that I won't even go there. As leaders, we have to be self-motivated, self-disciplined. The problem that we can face as people is that we wait until we feel like doing something before we do it, not realizing that if we do it we will feel good about it. That's why we need to reform our thinking. I have to eat right and exercise because it's the right thing to do. I have to keep myself on track with my personal goals and our corporate goals because that is the right direction to take.

If I feel before I act, I need to reform my thinking. I need to act, and then I will feel. I didn't feel like working out this morning. But after I did, I felt better than I have in a long time. Knowing that I need to motivate myself in order to develop my skills, I need to keep a plan to reform. If you are waiting for someone to motivate you, you might be waiting awhile. You need to lead yourself effectively before you can lead others.

3. My habit of doing too much too soon.

Since we are talking about change, or reformation, it is wise not to do too much all at once. I wanted to reform the grades I was getting my junior year at Taylor University. Shelley Chapin, a professor and friend, told me to choose the classes I would get one or two A's in. Then, choose the two or three classes I would get B's in. I wanted to shoot for straight A's, but she wisely counseled me to focus on a couple areas to change. Two things happened. I gave myself a goal I could reach, and I raised the level of all my grades by focusing on the one or two.

Keep a plan to perform

Once I have reformed my mind by realizing I am my greatest coach, I need to keep a plan of performing on a higher level. How do I keep myself performing at my peak?

1. Build on my strengths.

What are you strong in? For the most part, your areas of strength will be the areas you perform in most of the time. Spend most of your time developing your areas of strength. Make a plan that includes what you will read, what seminars you will attend, what tapes you may listen to in order to grow your strengths.

2. Get coached on my weaknesses.

We not only need to lead ourselves effectively, we should also look to a mentor for guidance. I was surprised by how many different coaches there were in football. They not only had the head coach and assistant coaches but also had running back coaches, quarterback coaches. Even though the players were operating in their areas of strength, they still needed coaching to help them develop. If people need encouragement in their areas of competence, we definitely need coaching in areas of weakness.

Coaching yourself, developing yourself, and being effective at motivating yourself will give you the fuel you will need to light the fires of those around you. As I keep my plan to reform my thinking and perform on a higher level, I then can motivate others by…

Developing reformers who push themselves from the inside

Help the people around you motivate themselves. The difference between intrinsic motivation and extrinsic motivation is that intrinsic comes from within. Extrinsic comes from outside. How do you get people to challenge themselves?

1. Bring on self-starters.

Hire people who lead themselves well. Before you hire them, get them to furnish proof of ways in which they had to motivate themselves to get something accomplished. Ask them whether they have had obstacles in their lives. What did they do to climb out of the hole, get out of the box, or drive over the bumps in the road of life?

2. Birth self-starters.

Develop people who will lead themselves well. My daughters Christina, Sierra and Rebecca didn't come out as self-starters. Even though they are very independent in a lot of ways, they didn't start out that way. They were very dependent. How do you develop people who will spur themselves on?

Laurence E. Anderson is the principal at Jacob Gunther Elementary School in North Bellmore, New York. Whether you are developing a young leader or a person who is new to leading themselves, Anderson suggests to "involve children in group activities." By bringing people together in collaborative teams, you can encourage them to solve problems and make decisions together.

Another way to develop them to lead themselves is to encourage public speaking opportunities. Little by little, you are helping people learn skills that they may have never developed. When you give them the opportunity to succeed, you help them feel better about themselves. This will get them used to taking initiative.

"I think teachers who delegate more and who have more innate trust and confidence in kids probably will see a larger percentage of those kids migrating into leadership roles," Anderson said.

A third way of developing self-leaders and self-motivators is to step away and permit them to have their independence. "Some of the people who gravitate toward leadership," Anderson continued, "on occasion will be people who may do something very contrary to the public outcry. They may be in the minority but be comfortable with that and not be terrified by it or paralyzed by it."[3]

And that's what you want. You want people who can stand on their own, yet work well with others. You want self-starters who can help start something in others. You want self-leaders who can lead others. And you want self-motivators who will motivate others.

Reward performers who push themselves and those around them

Coaches don't keep poor performers on their team, so why are you so afraid of loosing people? If you are loosing peak performers, then you've got a problem. Mick Delaney said, "any business or industry that pays equal rewards to its goof-offs and its eager beavers sooner or later will find itself with more goof-offs than eager beavers."

People who work hard are sometimes hounded by those who don't. "You'll make us look bad. Slow down," they say. Monetary rewards are always nice, but money is not the only way to motivate your team. Getting people to push each other is a great way to raise the level of excellence in your family, community or organization.

Delroy Calhoun felt negative pressure from his peers who "equated doing well in school with 'acting white.'" After Calhoun was kicked out of high school for fighting, he had to return back to school after everyone else had graduated. As he began to study, he realized how much he loved to learn. Growing through his tough experiences, Cal-

---

3.   Pryor, 32

houn is now promoting another form of peer pressure at the Bethlehem Center in Minneapolis.

Knowing that "preteens are most influenced by older teens, the Homework 'N' Hoops program has recently brought in a high school club of native Spanish speakers to tutor—and mentor—the younger children."[4]

Have the high performers in your organization encourage the others. What you expect is what you'll get.

> *"Who needs to be motivated in my circle of influence?"*
> *"What can I do to motivate them?"*

---

4.   Jacqueline White, "Delroy Calhoun Creates Community." *Assets Magazine,* Spring 1999, 12

11

Do the people around you feel needed?

○ ○
*"The biggest disease today is not leprosy or tuberculosis,
but rather the feeling of being unwanted, uncared for, and
deserted by everybody."*

—Mother Teresa

In his book, *Leadership Jazz,* Max DePree wrote about "a talented young woman with a bright future at Herman Miller." She "left one day, much to my surprise, to work for a competitor. Sadly I called to wish her the best, and she promised to write to me explaining her decision. After some weeks, I received a long letter describing her failure to find a different position in Herman Miller that would allow her to use her gifts, that would give her the chance to advance and to reach her potential. For me, the key sentence in her letter was 'I found several managers who said they wanted me, but nobody said they needed me.' There is indeed an important difference: In the workplace, to be needed is the crucial condition."[1]

---

1.   De Pree, 204

Define the feeling

The *Palm Beach Post* reported on outfielder Gary Sheffield's feelings of being unwanted. It's proof that money is not the key indicator in a person's happiness. After signing a six-year, $61 million deal, he still felt unwanted by the Marlin's owner.

"It's been a lot of tension," Sheffield told the Post. "Whenever you see Huizenga he makes a player feel uncomfortable. We say 'Hi' and 'Bye.' What would you think if you signed that kind of deal and the owner didn't talk to you?"

Feeling needed is something everyone needs, no matter whether you make $16,000 or $60,000. If you don't feel needed, you don't want to stay. Feeling needed means that you feel like you are indispensable to your family or organization. You are a necessary part of the team. People would feel like you left a hole if you were to leave. You are an essential part of what is going on.

Walk in their shoes

If you think that the ones who need to feel needed are the ones who have a lot of needs, here is another example of someone whose financial needs were met, but his need to be wanted went unmet.

In 1988, Danny Manning was the first overall pick in the NBA draft. Consensus player of the year at Kansas, Final Four MVP, and Olympian, Manning was 26 games into his rookie year with the Los Angeles Clippers when he suffered the first of three knee injuries in his career. Even though he had been haunted by injuries, Manning made two All-Star appearances, averaged more than 17 points and 6 rebounds per game, and was the NBA's 1998 Sixth Man Award winner. In his last season with the Suns he played all of their 50 games. No matter how much money or medals he has attained in his lifetime, when he doesn't feel needed by a team, it still hurts.

"Poor baby," you might be thinking. "I'd love to be in his over-sized basketball shoes," you say. No matter how many figures you pull in a year, you want to feel needed by the organization or family you belong to.

The period before the 1999-2000 season was pretty eventful for Manning. Within the course of three weeks, Manning was on three different teams. From Atlanta, Manning was brought on by Orlando. But Orlando advised him not to unpack.

"They told me not to get a house," Manning said. "I took that as a clue, sat back and waited for something to happen."

i-exam

When have I felt like I was a necessary part of an organization?
Did my parents make me feel like they needed me?
Do I feel like my talents are an essential part of this organization?
When have I felt like I was unnecessary?
Do I feel like there would be a hole if I were gone?
Who relies on me?

Develop the feeling

This whole discussion reminded me of a good friend I had back in college. Kris Fortuna never realized how needed she was to the street kids she was helping in Gas City, Indiana. I first met Kris when my band played at the storefront club she had for teens. Kids would come in, shoot pool, slam pop, and hang out. She provided a safe place for them to come.

Kris transferred her credits to Taylor University and graduated a year before me. It was then that she must have felt like she had nothing to work towards. I don't know what caused her to feel like an unnecessary part of this life, but on a Wednesday morning, it was announced to me and 1,500 other classmates after chapel that Kris was found dead in her apartment. Kris shot herself that morning.

I tried to do all I could. I had talked to her the Sunday before, and she said that she was doing better than she had in a long time. I was relieved, but my relief turned to sadness as I learned the news that Wednesday morning.

How do you make someone feel wanted? How do you let them know they are a necessary part of your life? How do you get them to believe it? I spent time with Kris. I counseled her on what seemed to be very dark thoughts. We had a circle of friends, so I know that Kris had a network of people who cared about her.

And I guess that's the thing. You can't **make** someone feel a certain way. There are no guarantees that someone will feel needed, appreciated, or important. But when we take specific actions, we will help more people around us feel that way.

Tell them…specifically

There have been so many people in my life that have caused me to feel like I was a necessary part of my family, my school, my church, and my community. My parents, even my grandparents helped me to believe in myself. Everyone needs that kind of support.

"What you do is so critical to our operations. Let me tell you how." Think through some questions. Who is needed to make this family or organization work? When are they needed? Why are they necessary? What is it about her that makes her critical to you? Where is he needed? How are they needed? Once you have gone through all those questions, you are then able to tell them specifically why you need them.

Show them…repeatedly

Some people feel like they are an unnecessary part of an organization when they are no longer challenged. The "talented young woman at Herman Miller" wanted to find another job within the company where she could use her gifts more effectively. Giving people jobs that are a necessary part of the organization help them feel needed as well. Sure they wanted her around, but they didn't show her that her specific skills were needed. Show them how critical they are to you by giving them work that challenges them to grow. Let them see for themselves what they can do when they are used to their full potential.

Who needs to feel needed around me?
What can I do today to help them feel that way?

12

Do the people around you feel safe and secure?

o o o o o o o o o o o o o o o o o o o o o o o o o o o o o o
"It is difficult to give children a sense of security unless you have it yourself. If you have it, they catch it from you."

—Dr. William C. Menninger

There really is more to fear than fear itself. When I was younger, I bet I could have joined the Olympic Track & Field Team for my long jumps. There was no way that thing underneath my bed was going to get me. And you had better believe I wasn't going to let my hand go over the edge of the bed either. No telling what was under my bed that could rip my hand off in a split second.

I wish that was all we had to fear.

- 100% of couples who marry want it to last forever. Over 50% of marriages split.

- 100% of children want to be close to their parents. 15.8 million kids now live in single-parent households, with one in four growing up without a father in the home.

- 100% of kids want to grow up in a safe home. An average of 100,000 teens are homeless every day.

- 100% of teens want to feel good about themselves. Two million try to kill themselves each year, with more than 6,000 succeeding.

We no longer simply fear the dark. We fear each other. We are reluctant to have intimacy that goes deeper than sex. You read that right. Emotional intimacy is deeper than physical intimacy, especially in a world that treats sex so cheaply. We are afraid to let down our guard.

We are hesitant to try new things. The dying words of companies and congregations alike are "we've never done it that way before." Risk? Forget it. Too dangerous.

Everyone wants to be safe. They want to feel secure, but many have never felt the touch of a protective father or mother. Everyone wants to have a rewarding career with people they get along with, but many grudgingly go to work with people they can't stand. Many of us have come up with ideas that would help our companies or our families, but risking the discomfort of rocking the boat, we keep silent.

Define the feeling

There's a difference between being a peacemaker and being a peacekeeper. Peacemakers will make peace at any cost. Peacekeepers will keep the peace at any cost. Peacemakers may rock the boat, stir the water, or afflict the comfortable. Peacekeepers will try to control the boat, settle the water, or comfort the afflicted. What's the difference?

The difference between the two is their source for safety and security. For the peacekeeper, his source of security is outside of himself. It's keeping everyone else happy. It's meeting everyone else's expectations. For the peacemaker, her source of safety is inside. It's doing what's right no matter what everybody else thinks. It's being true to yourself. It's being honest with yourself. It's living with integrity. It's being the same person in private as you are in public. It's being the same person in public as you are in private.

If being safe and secure means to be sturdy and strong, protected from risk or harm, does that mean the peacemaker keeps from being a risk-taker? If you are trying to help others feel secure around you, does that mean you don't challenge them to get out of their comfort zone? How do you balance the two?

Walk in their shoes

One of our former homes was an apartment complex that had a commons area in the center of five buildings. Our girls could play outside in a huge sandbox (a.k.a. the sand volleyball court) or on the jungle gym. There was a spiral slide, a small slide, and a pole to slide down. Both Christy and Sierra felt safe going down either slide, but Christy wanted go down the pole.

At first she didn't want to go on her own. She was afraid. She felt unsafe. Insecure. If I were a peacekeeper, I'd tell her not to go down the pole. It's too dangerous. It's risky. She might get hurt.

She might, but she also might grow in the way she thinks about herself if she overcomes a fear. Courage is not the absence of fear. Courage is walking through your fears. As a peace-making father, I told her step-by-step what she should do.

At first she wanted to sit down, but sitting would not allow her to reach the pole. She had to stretch out with her whole body. That's fine when you are a foot off the ground, but when you are a three-footer yourself looking six feet down, it can be intimidating.

"Hold the side with one hand and reach out with the other," I told her. "Once you have a hold of the pole, reach out with your other hand. Hold the pole tight as you swing your legs around the pole." I stood right below her, guiding each arm and leg until she felt comfortable herself. After only a few times of doing it with me, she was able to conquer her fear and do it all on her own. The next day she showed Sierra how to do it.

i-exam

What scares you? When have you felt uneasy, insecure, unsafe?
What is the difference between physical and emotional security?
What specifically scared you in the past, and what got you through it?
Who helped you get through your fears and what did they do?

Develop the feeling

The scene with Christy out in the back yard can be translated any-where. Everyday, there are people around you that are afraid of some-thing. They may even be afraid of you. If you get any pleasure out of that statement, you have a problem. You want people to respect you as a leader, but you do not want them to fear you. We need to protect the people around us, but we also need to provide them with the tools to work through their fears.

Provide, don't just protect

If your job were just to protect people from harm, they would not grow. Your job is to help them risk safely. There are people you deal with everyday that need to risk, but won't take the leap unless you can help them risk safely. Provide an environment where the people around you can feel free to take the risk.

Dancing with the feelings of freedom and safety is a delicate job, but there might be times when you need to step on some toes. In this envi-ronment of risk, of helping people find the courage to work through their fears, you need to provide a relationship where you stand under-neath them as they are reaching out to new poles. You need to coach them, giving them suggestions about what their next step can be. Bet-ter yet, if you can guide them as they discover new ways of reaching out, they will grow to rely on themselves even more.

Understand

"It is a wise father that knows his own child."
—William Shakespeare

"Emotional protection is far less visible or predictable than physical protection," Robert Wolgemuth wrote. "It may change in form as the years go by, but it's just as important as physical protection. Be as available as you can. Always let your daughter's call through. Wear a pager or carry a cellular phone. If you're not there the moment she needs you, she'll find someone else—possibly someone whose wisdom is inferior to yours."

The first thing you need to understand is the person. Wolgemuth's book, *She Calls Me Daddy*, helped me realize that raising girls is a lot different than raising boys. I grew up in a family of boys, and I now have three girls. I am realizing that I need to understand the needs of each of them as much as possible, so that I can help them grow in ways that match who they are as individuals.

Find out what they fear. Ask them the questions you asked yourself during your *i-exam*. Ask them what scares them. What is unsettling to them in your organization or your family. Then discover ways to help them grow through their fears.

The second thing to understand is that there are different phases of fear. Some people have physical fears, fearing for their safety. Others have emotional or social fears, where they fear getting too close to people. Some may have vocational fears. They don't speak in front of people well. Understanding the person and the phases of fear will help you to provide for and protect those around you. How do you do it?

Let your life be full of love

If you have ever been to a funeral, you have probably heard the 23rd Psalm. David was a songwriter as well as the King of Israel. I questioned his lyrics one day, and I quickly got an answer.

He wrote, "Even when I walk through the valley of the shadow of death, I will fear no evil; For You are with me; Your rod and Your staff, they comfort me. You prepare a table before me in the presence of my enemies; You anoint my head with oil; My cup runs over..."

What does that mean, "My cup runs over?" I thought to myself, "That's a waste." And then I realized something. It is only a waste if I don't pour it into the lives of other people. And you can only pour it into the lives of people if you have it yourself.

You have to have a sense of security in order to give it away. If you are not secure in who you are, you may have a difficult time helping someone else feel secure. If you are not secure, hang out with people who are. If you are not confident, spend time with those who are. Spend more of your time, if not all of your time, with people who will lift you up instead of tear you down.

Let your home be a haven of rest

I not only want my home to be a safe place for my own wife and children, but I also want it to be a place where my neighbors and their children can let down their guard. Whenever there's a storm, you usually head inside. I want my home to be a place where people can weather life's storms. During the most difficult times in my life, I have had other homes to go to for emotional shade and shelter. Ask your family how you can provide that to them as well as their friends.

We may think of rest as going to sleep. When things aren't going right in your life, the first thing that goes is usually a good night's sleep. Let your home be a place where people can rest themselves—physically, emotionally, mentally. Provide them a place where they can rest their bodies, minds, and souls.

Let your friendship be a fortress of peace

People in my community were asked by The Barna Research Group, "Where do you turn for help when dealing with significant problems?"

Seventy-seven percent of the respondents said friends or family. Are you known as someone others can confide in? Are you someone the people around you can trust? Do your friends know you will hold them accountable if they get off track? Do you care enough to confront a person who is going in a direction that will hurt herself or her family?

From the first time I spent time with Michelle, I could tell something was different. If peace means serenity, silence, and stillness, I could tell that being friends with her was going to be peaceful. We talk a lot, but during that first time of hanging out together, we were able to be with each and not have to say anything. Peace's opposite is agitation, disturbance. As a friend, provide a relationship where the people around you can be silent. Calm them. Don't disturb them. Quiet them. Don't agitate them.

Let your work be a wall of protection

You may have a firewall protecting your information technology. You might have security access at every entrance. Security cameras might be strategically placed throughout your warehouse. You may even have security guards. All of these are measures to protect your information, equipment, or employees' lives.

Take measures that will also protect your people emotionally. When you challenge them, let them know what they are doing right as well. When you give them more responsibilities, give them the resources they need to succeed. When you talk to them about their professional performance, find out if there is anything you can do for them personally. Make them feel emotionally secure just as much as they feel physically stable.

Do the people around me feel safe and secure?
What can I do today to give someone a sense of security?

13

How significant do the people around you feel?

o o o o o o o o o o o o o o o o o o o o o o o o o o o o o o o o o

"At the very heart of leadership lies the necessity of making it possible for followers to contribute." [1]

We have opportunities everyday to make a difference in the lives of other people. I love surprising the drivers behind me by paying their way on a toll road. The look of surprise on their faces is great.

James Briscoe is a courier for Federal Express who treats the customers on his route just like he was running his own business.

"If I were running a business, I'd want customers to *feel* that they were dealing with somebody who is friendly, professional, and helpful. Just last week, a customer stopped me on the street and asked me how to reach our main office by subway. She'd left her home for a short time and had missed a really important delivery, so our office was holding a package for her. I told her that if she could wait, I'd deliver it to her door the very next day.

"But she needed the package by noon that day," Briscoe continued. "She didn't have a car, and she was new to the area. I thought about how complicated it would be for her to take the subway and then walk the rest of the way to our office. So I told her to give me 15 minutes,

---

1. De Pree, 110

and I would get the package and be right back with it. You can imagine how happy she was.

"But I didn't help her out because I was looking for a pat on the back. I just did what I could to help a customer in a tough situation. You want to do the right thing for people. You want to put yourself in their shoes, as if you were the one asking for help. Part of customer service is the great *feeling* that you get when you see that you've made a difference."[2]

We all have a need to feel significant, like we are making a contribution to society, and we don't have to wait until our shift is over to make that happen.

Define the feeling

We've tasted success as leaders. Have you ever tasted significance? Would you have expected teenagers to take their Spring Break to do anything but party? Thousands do it every year, and I had the privilege of working side by side with some of them.

Sam Simons was a senior that year. It was her senior trip, but instead of going to Cancun, Aruba, or Hawaii, she went to Juarez, Mexico. Instead of sleeping in a nice hotel room overlooking the ocean, she stayed with 13 other people in a gated church facility, sleeping with that same group in the sanctuary of the church.

"Instead of going to Cancun or some other party spot," Sam wrote, "I came here to build a house. I would not have wanted to do anything else. Doing a mission trip is so much more rewarding than any party could be. By not going to Cancun, I took a lot of heat from my fellow classmates about wasting my time. But that is so not true. I've learned so much about myself and 13 other people that had I gone to Cancun, I probably wouldn't remember anything that happened."

"There is no other feeling like you get when you serve others in need," Jenny Weaks said. She was a junior in high school when we

2.   McCauley, pp 93.

went. "This week we learned so much about other people and how to serve others unselfishly. We couldn't even speak the same language as the people we built the house for, but we learned to communicate through hand signals and gestures. It brought us all very close together. It's a rare opportunity for people to get to go on a mission trip like this but I wish so many more people would make the time and effort to go. When you get the chance, I hope you take it. You won't regret it!"

Feeling like you are important has more to do with who you are. Feeling significant has more to do with what you are doing with your life. You live your life for others instead of just yourself. You look out for the interests of others, not just your own. It's giving more than money. It's giving yourself to your family, your friends, your clients and co-workers. Success is great, but significance is meaningful.

In *Leading With Soul*, Maria asked Steve, "How can you have it all and have nothing?"[3] She helped Steve realize that "the gift of significance lets people find meaning in work, faith in themselves, confidence in the value of their lives, and hope for the future."[4]

Walk in their shoes

Walk in the shoes of another teen: "It was great. We had so much fun," said Scott Richardson, who was 13 at the time. What he noticed was how the team's relationships seemed to deepen as they learned to make a significant difference in the lives of others.

"Our relationships between each other were great. We came to know each other better. We talked to each other a lot more. Even though we might get angry or frustrated, we just helped each other out. When we were finished and dedicating the home to the family, you're just so happy that you're finished, and that you've built a home for a homeless person or family."

---

3.   Bolman and Deal, 93
4.   Bolman and Deal, 113

Scott and the other teens found significance in the children they played with after a hard days work.

"The church that we stayed in was great, because there were little kids there to play with. Even though we didn't speak much Spanish, we still communicated with them. These experiences have been a great part of my life and I do plan on going again and again."

"There is a deep human yearning to make a difference. We want to know that we've done something on this earth that our life means something. We want to know that there's a purpose to our existence."[5]

i-exam

When have I made a difference in someone's life? How did that make me feel?

Who has made the greatest impact on me and what did they do?

What difference would it make in my life if I strive for significance just as hard as I strive for success?

Develop the feeling

At the heart of this chapter is not only the idea of us making a difference in the lives of others, but also the idea of making it possible for the people around us to make a difference. How can we help others become successful *and* significant?

---

5.   Kouzes and Posner, 132

Encourage the people around you to go M.A.D. (make a difference)...

...at home.

How can we help the people in our home make a difference? Right after Christina was born, some families from our church organized to provide us food for the coming weeks. Each family cooked a meal in a throwaway pan, usually big enough to feed us a few nights. Each family brought a meal at different times throughout week.

As a family you can sponsor a child in this or another country. You can provide a Thanksgiving meal for a family who might not be able to afford it. You can take your family out to purchase gifts for a needy family in your neighborhood for Christmas. Whatever you do, organize times for your family to make a difference in the lives of others.

...in your community.

How can we help the people in our communities taste significance? As a part of the Kiwanis Club, we took families shopping for Christmas. We "warmed the children" by organizing a coat drive. We started a KEY Club so that we could help students make a difference in their school and community. Whether you are involved with a church or civic organization, organize the people in your community to make a difference from around the corner to around the world.

...at work in the lives of your clients.

Help the people you work with go the extra mile in their relationships with their clients and customers. James Briscoe realized he could make a difference in the life of a customer. There were so many businesses in our area that gave donations to our efforts at church and through Kiwanis. If your company is doing that, I commend you and thank you for all you do. Go the extra step of giving your employees the opportunity to do something for the community you serve in. Help them get their hands dirty.

...at work in the lives of your community.

When the "Grinch tried to steal Christmas" in Dallas, the people of Southwest Airlines made sure he couldn't steal the happiness of the children who would have received the toys. Hearing that a Salvation Army truck filled with gifts for needy children had been stolen, "Ken Gile, then an assistant chief pilot for Southwest, walked into Gary Barron's office and said, 'I need $5,000 today.' Gile told Barron what had happened and promised that he would lead the charge to raise the money to repay the company." Gile then rounded up other employees, took off in a pickup, and went shopping. "By the time they returned with a truckload of three hundred toys to deliver to the Salvation Army that afternoon, other employees had raised over $5,000."[6]

> **"What little thing can I do today to make a difference in someone's life?"**
> **"What could I do to help organize an effort to make a difference?"**

---

6.   Kevin & Jackie Freiberg, *Nuts! Southwest Airlines' Crazy Recipe for Business and Personal Success* (New York: Broadway Books, 1996, 1997), 236

14

Do the people around you feel like you trust them?

I met Julie Ryan, author of *Defending Your Digital Assets,* one night at the Spring Lecture Series presented by Eastern Michigan University in 2000. Julie Ryan advises clients on information security through her Wyndrose Technical Group. What surprised me was the prevalence of problems that comes from company insiders—you know—the people you are supposed to trust with information.

I used to work for a company that installed security cameras. The installs that I was involved in were overt. We installed them during the day, mainly to make companies and parking lots safer. Some of the installs that the company did, though, were covert operations. They had to be installed when the company or business was closed because management believed their own employees were stealing resources from the company.

In this day when we have to be so cautious, how do we develop an atmosphere of trust in our companies? How do you trust someone when at the same time you have to worry about information security?

Define the feeling

When you trust someone you are showing that you have confidence in his or her abilities. Being trustworthy means that you are worthy of someone's trust. You are dependable. People are able to depend on you. You are reliable. Your friends are able to rely on you. You are loyal and devoted. People place their faith in you.

When you shatter that trust, people begin to doubt you. It may even take some time to regain that trust. Optimists can be turned into pessimists very easily if they get burned enough. Guarding the trust and confidence people place in you is the best thing to keep secure.

Walk in their shoes

On the second day of building the home in Mexico, our team leader from Casas Por Cristo left us in order to pick up some more supplies. Usually they would call to have them delivered, but Mike Scott did something that surprised the kids. He left.

"He left us to do the work?" the kids asked. "That's really cool. He must trust us with doing a good job on the house." Mike realized where our team was at in our development. Half of us were returning for our second year. Barry was a gifted carpenter. Mike laid out the plan, got us started, and then left in order to get us some more water. His actions made the kids feel like he could rely on them to do a good job without him being there.

i-exam

When was the first time someone trusted in my abilities?
How did it feel when they placed their confidence in me?
Have I ever lost confidence in someone? What was it like trying to trust them again?

Have I ever lost the faith someone placed in me? What did it take for me to regain that trust in their eyes?

How am I at trusting others with their work?

Develop the feeling

Craftsman Custom Metal Fabricators in Illinois had half of its business wrapped-up with Motorola in the late 1980s. So what was Bruce Bendoff's company going to do when Motorola announced it would "pair down its supplier base and turn the survivors into partners?"

"It all came down to the word trust," Bendoff told *Inc. Magazine*. Bendoff began to see his trust of Motorola pay off. The two companies collaborated on parts designs, the time to production dropped. "Something that took five weeks before," Bendoff continued, "could now be produced in literally one or two days."

Jordan Lewis, a consultant based in Washington, D.C., calls relationships like that of Craftsman and Motorola "alliance relationships." I call them reliance relationships.

How do you develop a reliance relationship between you and another company? How do you build trust between you and your customers, you and your co-workers? What can families and friends do in building stronger relationships of trust?

Communicate clearly and specifically

Craftsman engineer Al Krempels leads seminars to help build trust at clients' sites. "The customer is starting to realize that to get good parts, it needs to get us good information," Krempels said.

Be worthy of their trust first

Throughout its history, Craftsman has had to help its customers overcome their fear of commitment. Krempels told *Inc.*, "it took 18 months for one customer to come around. We have to be the initiator."

Plan for the worst...

When trust breaks down, "I can almost bet money that there's an ego issue behind it," Bendoff said. He strongly believes "egotists should be reeducated, booted, or made to wear buttons with a red slash through the word ego."[1]

A company's main enemy may not be hackers from the outside, but inflated egos from the inside. You have to guard the relationships you have with your people. You bring Julie Ryan in to assist you in securing your information. You can also hire people to assist you in strengthening the relationships of the people in your company.

"The threats you have to consider are natural and active," Ryan told her audience. Natural threats are related to weather or earthquakes, sometimes known as "acts of God." Great distinction isn't it? How would you like to be known as the one who initiates destruction? The other threat is active, which usually comes through human initiative. Computer bugs are non-human active threats, though they obviously started with a human.

"A person who is an active threat to your company has to have the capability and the intent," Ryan said. If you have the ability to act but don't intend to, then there won't be any problem. If you have the intent but do not have the capability, you can't act. Ryan told her audience that you can't protect yourself from all threats, but you can set a plan in motion that will eliminate most of them. She can consult you on the technology available to do so.[2] Let me consult you on the personal resources you have to do so. It's called expecting the best from people.

---

1. Inc. june 1, 1997
2. Julie Ryan, *Defending Your Digital Assets* (New York: McGraw Hill, 2000)

...but expect the best.

So the people in your business have the capability to do you and your company harm. How do you keep them from intending to do harm? You place more interest in them personally than you would professionally. Be concerned about their development. Give them every reason to do their best for you. When someone is truly concerned about them personally and places faith in them, more times then not, they will live up to those expectations.

Who do I need to place more trust in today?
What can I do to help them have confidence in themselves?

15

Do the people around you feel like you understand them?

○ ○

"Instead of putting others in their place, put yourself in their place."

—anonymous

L.L. Bean takes walking in someone's shoes to a whole new level. Elizabeth Spaulding, as Vice President of Customer Satisfaction at L.L. Bean, knows that at the foundation of customer service lies customer understanding.

"If a customer calls and wants to return a Maine Hunting Shoe," Spaulding said, "the first thing we do is find out what that customer's expectations were when buying the shoe. Did she expect it to last 10 years? If the answer is yes, then there's no question: We'll replace the shoe. If it turns out that she expected it to last only one year, then we'll repair the shoe. The point is that the customer determines the expectation. Not us."

Spaulding has found her customers to be totally honest when it comes to their expectations. "They're just like your neighbors," Spaulding said. "And when you realize that your customers are just like you, the whole dynamic of your interaction with them changes."[1]

---

1.   McCauley, pp 93.

Define the feeling

"Give every man thine ear, but few thy voice."
—*Shakespear*

The essence of understanding is that the people around you, like it or not, are just like you. When you are trying to understand someone, you are trying to feel what they feel, experience what they experience, and think how they think. When you understand someone, you are trying to comprehend where they are coming from. It's more than hearing. It's listening. It's discerning. It's more than looking. It's seeing. It's realizing.

There's a difference between understanding and standing over. Try this as an illustration. When you are talking to someone, stand over them. How does it make you feel? Have that same person stand over you. Now how does it make you feel? Understanding is not so much physical posturing as it is emotional. When you understand someone, you are assuming a position of humility, literally standing under them.

Walk in their shoes

"When you walk in the shoes of another,
be sure not to step on their feet."

That is really the definition of understanding: walking in their shoes. How often do you seek the truth from their point of view?

"What I do best is read people's feelings," Lynn Wilde told me. While on the set of The Best Christmas Pageant Ever, Lynn realized that one of her youngest actresses was feeling down. Lynn walked over to her and asked how she was doing. She told Lynn, "I don't know where I need to be." Lynn replied, "On my lap." She climbed up as Lynn continued to direct the rehearsal. If anyone leaves the rehearsal feeling like something went wrong, Lynn knows it and gives them a call to see how they are doing. Understanding people is one of the greatest qualities leaders have. Leaders not only know where they are going, but know where people are coming from.

i-exam

When have I truly been understood?
Who best understands me and why?
What do they do to comprehend where I am coming from?
How am I at understanding the needs of others?

Develop the feeling

"Natural talent, intelligence, a wonderful education—none of these guarantees success. Something else is needed:
The sensitivity to understand what other people want and the willingness to give it to them."
—John Luther

One of the books that profoundly influenced me was Covey's *Seven Habits of Highly Effective People*. One of those habits was to "seek first to understand, then to be understood." How do you understand where people are coming from?

Keep your eyes attentive

When you are talking to someone, keep your eyes on them. Whether you have the ability to do two things at once doesn't matter. If you are not looking at them, they will think you have something else on your mind. Making eye contact with them will help you…

Keep your mind focused

This tends to be more of a difficulty if you are task-oriented. Your mind more naturally goes to things you have to accomplish. I personally need people like you around me, because you are more focused on the details of the organization. But you have to be available to people. It will be more of a struggle to keep your mind focused on the person in front of you instead of the task at hand. Keeping the voices in your head quiet will help you…

Keep your ears open

Covey wrote, listen with the intent to understand. Don't listen with the intent to reply. Keep from thinking of what you are going to say next. We are sometimes more interested in winning an argument and defending our case. When that happens, we are listening to ourselves more than we are listening to them. Keeping your ears open will allow you to…

Keep your mouth shut

I really don't like this one. I have something to say about everything. But I need to exercise the gift of having two ears. The only time you want to open your mouth when you are attempting to understand is when you want to clarify an issue. It's called "drive-through window" communication. Once you have told Mc. Burger Bell your order, they repeat what they think they heard you say. Once you clarify what was just said, they can tell you whether you heard them right.

Keep your arms open

Sometimes people don't choose the most opportune times to talk. Make the time for them, keeping your door and your arms open. Maybe you have to work out a better time, telling them that you really want to hear what they have to say, but need to schedule it when you can give them more of your time and attention.

Keep your feet moving

"In such (a global) environment, it's vital to manage employees properly, helping them adapt to new markets and sensitizing them to new cultures," said J.P. Donlon. This task is somewhat easier if a company has managers and employees who have lived in and understand other countries."[2]

People who give simple answers to complex issues have not been around the block, let alone out of their box. Understanding where people are coming from helps when you've been there yourself. If you come from a divorced home, you know what other children have experienced. If you have had someone close to you die, you know what it feels like. If you need someone to understand your market in Malaysia, you are better off finding someone who knows the language, the culture and the traditions.

> *"Most people fail or succeed on their ability to know and understand the people they work with."*
> *—Russ Barnett, proprieter of Russell Marketing*

> *Who do I need to make time for today?*

---

2. J.P. Donlon, "CE Roundtable: Three Pillars of Globalization," *Chief Executive,* September 1996, 61

Conclusion

◆

Keeping Your Eyes Open

I had an opportunity to have lunch with Tony Terlato and some of his staff at his home overlooking the Napa Valley. From the time I stepped into the house I could tell there was something special about him.

Tony is chairman and CEO of the Terlato Wine Group, which is the holding company for the Terlato family of businesses. It includes Paterno Wines International, which has become the leading marketer of premium wines in the United States. The Wine Spectator honored him as one of 18 industry leaders that shaped the wine industry over the past 20 years.

I first heard about Tony as I walked around Rutherford Hill Winery with Willis Blakewell, general manager of the winery. He couldn't say enough about what the Terlatos brought when they purchased the winery in 1996. In that first year Tony worked with Rutherford's winemakers to eliminate 14,000 cases of wine from their first blend. They wanted to guarantee that the 1995 vintage of Rutherford Hill Napa Valley Merlot was consistent with the family philosophy of quality first.

Quality relationships

That quality first mentality was something I saw in his relationships. Within two minutes of walking through the kitchen door that day, Tony had his apron on and put me to work stirring the sauce. I was going there to interview him for an article when I found myself feeling like I was hanging out with a friend.

Willis Blakewell could not say enough about Tony and his leadership at Rutherford. His staff at lunch bragged on him as a person who they enjoyed working for. A visitor to my church was surprised to find out that I knew Tony personally. Dave Scott had been working for Tony for years heading up sales in the west and called Tony a second father.

Quality relationships extended into his family and friendships. When I visited Tony at his home in Indian Wells, near Palm Springs, California, there were pictures everywhere of friends he enjoyed being with and family he loved bragging on. He couldn't say enough about his own kids, who were working with him in the business. He talked non-stop about his grandchildren, and how he was instilling in them the same work ethic that made him successful.

And there was his relationship with Jojo, his wife. It doesn't take long to realize how much a husband and wife love each other. It is seen in the looks they give one another or the way they speak to each other.

The warmth in the friendships he had while playing a round of golf at his home in Indian Wells was evident as well. These were other industry leaders who simply enjoyed being together. And as I rode in their custom golf carts made to look like their favorite car, I found something very interesting. They talked more about the relationships with those around them than the accomplishments of their leadership.

Tony said relationships have a lot to do with chemistry.

"I'm comfortable with you. You're comfortable with me. There is no stress between us. It doesn't always happen that way, but when it happens you grow the relationship." Tony has been growing relationships for years and reaping the benefits of his efforts.

The efforts he places in his family and corporate relationships extends to his partnerships. As he talked about his partnership with winemaker Michel Laroche, he said "we were huggin' each other after ten minutes because we found something very special. And it wasn't based on economics or numbers of cases."

John Maxwell is right. It is only lonely at the top if you don't bring anyone with you.

Making them feel a part of the vision

"When I came here in 1996 the first thing I did was to have a poster made of an important wine magazine and I put Rutherford Hill on the front cover," Tony said. "It read, 'the best Merlot in California.' I put the date on the magazine as September 2, 2002. I told them that I would give them six years to accomplish that and you start tomorrow."

He told them "you don't have to guess where I want to be. Tell me what it takes to get there. I'll provide you with everything it takes to get there. Everybody has it hanging in their offices. I won't accept not to make a better wine every year. So don't find excuses of rain or sun or anything. Make less, but make it good. The first vintage we had we did the tasting. We eliminated 14,000 cases out of the blend. You have to bite the bullet sooner or later. At that time they were producing 86,000 cases. Everybody there understood I wasn't kidding. I wasn't asking them to do the impossible and then tie their hands behind their back. We tasted the wines and everything that wasn't good got cut out of the blend."

Making them feel important

Tony tells his managers to hire the best people possible. He says that "B" and "C" class managers don't hire "A" class managers, but "A's" do hire other "A's." They also raise the leadership levels of those around them from "B's" to "A's". They're not afraid of hiring people who are as good as them or better.

When I asked him who made him realize he was an "A" he humbly admitted, "I don't even know if I am an "A." His staff disagreed, arguing how they felt like they were better leaders and people because the influence of Tony on their lives.

"I think the people that entrusted me with their brands made me have a feeling that I was moving in the right direction," Tony admitted. "I only have quality on my mind. Those are the people I want to be with."

Eyes wide open

In my conversations with people about the way they feel working for someone, I have seen the need to develop better working relationships. I have been with kids who either feel good about themselves or are down on themselves because of the way they have been treated at home.

Patty Magro is a close friend and a teacher here in Napa. It drives her crazy to see teachers who don't love their kids. It's evident in the looks they give and the way they talk to their students.

Wherever you are, whatever you are doing, the way you treat the people around you will be evident in the success of your business and personal lives. It is up to us to keep our eyes wide open in order to focus on deepening the relationships around us.

Whether you're at home or at work, don't forget to look at it this way.

About the Author

John E. Aho works for Young Life and Redwood Community Church and holds a BA in Psychology from Taylor University and a Masters of Divinity from Golden Gate Seminary. He has written hundreds of articles for *Insider Business Journal and Vineyard & Winery Management.* He and his wife Michelle live in Napa, CA with their three daughters. He can be contacted at www.LeadershipJourney.com.

0-595-28914-2